Gracious

A Practical Primer on Charm, Tact, and Unsinkable Strength*

*Including instructions on being kind when you don't feel like it,
ignoring the Internet and/or disarming trolls,
and generally staying serene and sensible in a world that is neither*

Kelly Williams Brown

New York Times bestselling author of *Adulting*

RODALE.

Mention of specific companies, organizations, or authorities in this book does not imply endorsement by the author or publisher, nor does mention of specific companies, organizations, or authorities imply that they endorse this book, its author, or the publisher.

Internet addresses and telephone numbers given in this book were accurate at the time it went to press.

Rodale books may be purchased for business or promotional use or for special sales. For information, please write to: Special Markets Department, Rodale Inc., 733 Third Avenue, New York, NY 10017.

Printed in the United States of America

Rodale Inc. makes every effort to use acid-free ⊗, recycled paper ♲.

Book design by Christina Gaugler

Illustrations by Kelly Williams Brown

Library of Congress Cataloging-in-Publication Data is on file with the publisher.

ISBN-13: 978–1–62336–797–8

Distributed to the trade by Macmillan

2   4   6   8   10   9   7   5   3   1   hardcover

To the Bloxom women—
Georgia, GB, Elaine, Phyllis, Barbie, Olivia, and Elizabeth

Help us to be aware
Of the words we are called to speak,
Of the actions we are called to take part in,
Of the compassion we are called to offer
In a world so wounded, so in need.

—Prayer for Mindfulness

Always stay gracious;
best revenge is your paper.

—Beyoncé, "Formation"

Contents

Introduction

In which we explore how flower arrangements can (maybe, possibly) save the world

ello, gentle reader! I am *so* delighted you're here—or there, I suppose, in a bookstore or on your couch or squished in an airplane seat. More importantly, I hope you are well, that you are living in a world more lovely and kind than the one in which I write these words.

This world is . . . well . . . (*deep breath*) not always great, y'all. It's not great. There is so much yelling at each other, and when we're not yelling, it's because we're ignoring one another. We're more comfortable making constant, prolonged eye contact with our phones than with each other. Also, there's genocide; that's a thing we do, too.

If the world were a person, I might possibly even go so far as to drop the atomic bomb of Southern disapproval. "Y'all," I would say, lowering my voice and glancing around to make sure no one would overhear this verbal execution, "you know what I think? I think its mamma *didn't raise it right*," and everyone would nod solemnly. The world would then be dead to us.

Humans are social animals, and sometimes we feel a collective emotion. Unfortunately, that emotion is more often fear or despair or loneliness in a room full of people and not, say, excitement that we (as humanity) are all going boating together this afternoon *and* Allyson is bringing enough cheese and Trader Joe's prosciutto for all.

We knit back together at times, usually tragic, for a little while, then resume standard operating procedure: retreating from the humans around us and returning our gaze to our screens. Oh, I love a good screen. I do! It's *embarrassing* how much time I spend looking at them. My screens tell me about all the wonderful and terrible things that are happening in the world and to my closest friends, the achievements of people I barely know, the ugly things people are saying. In return, I tell my screens how angry I am, then smugly tally who agrees with me. Screens contain everything in the world, it seems (except what is actually physically around me), and, most importantly, I can use these screens to tell *other* screens about myself.

We dedicate so much time and energy to making sure the world is aware of us—look, here's a picture of my breakfast! I exist! Just a quick Snapchat to remind you that I am a human! Here are my thoughts on that stupid thing someone said on Twitter! I take up physical space and matter in the universe and my opinions matter, I like to think.

The world, per always, remains indifferent to us, and yet we take it so *personally.* And this bit of existential dissonance is reinforced constantly as we move through life indifferent to the humans around us.

We view the people right in front of us as lumbering obstacles preventing us from moving down a sidewalk; logistical and social traffic jam that must be dealt with on the way to the things that actually matter.

This, at least, is *my* default. While this interpretation of humanity may be, in some sense, technically correct, there is a difference between correct and true.

But here's the problem with that kind of thinking: Every human is *just as human as you are.* They, like you, want—perhaps even *need*—to be acknowledged. They came from somewhere and are going somewhere, too. They did not begin existing at the moment you heard their stupid ringtone on the bus and the even more irritating conversation that followed. Nor will they cease to exist, dissolving like sidewalk chalk in the rain, once they are out of your earshot.

Though it is very (very) easy to assume otherwise, each person you will ever encounter is just as much in their own head as you are in yours. They, like you, have things like a favorite food, a lucky pencil, a childhood pet whose loss, to this day, still can give them a lump in their throat. They have a happiest moment of their life, that beautiful day or hour of perfection they keep wrapped and packed away in their mind. They, like you, pull out this memory to buffer themselves against present pain and distractions, to remember that things were once okay, better than okay, that they were once sublimely happy and may be again one day.

This person, this Other, who is not inside your head and will never understand what it means to live your life, has also experienced the worst day of their life. In fact, *today might even be that day.* How would you know?

All we can do is follow Kurt Vonnegut's advice: "There's only one rule that I know of, babies—God damn it, you've got to be kind."

Manners! It's a small, everyday word that encapsulates *so terrifically much!* Good manners encompass sincere compassion, kindness, and respect—not as something to be doled out when you feel like it or want to impress someone, but as your baseline. Bad manners consist of . . . well* . . . as Ludwig Wittgenstein said, "That which we cannot speak of, we must pass over in silence."

Making this the foundation upon which we build every human

---

* Here, please note the first example of the Gracious Lady Way to Sh*t-Talk: You bring up a subject, give a little shudder, then imply that whatever it is is simply *too* awful to even *think* about, let alone *talk about,* though you may then expressively dwell on the topic. One of my very favorite people in the world, my godmother, is a reigning champion of this kind of talk: "I mean, my GOD, it's like a *terrible nightmare that we are all living in!* Part of me wants to scream about it from the treetops just to *warn* everyone, like a deranged *Paul Revere* or whatever, and the *other* part of me is just ready to slit my damn *wrists* and lie down to wait for *death,*" and it turns out that she's talking about the dearth of good Vietnamese restaurants in her small, rural town.

interaction is the only antidote I know of for that pervasive loneliness I mentioned earlier. Occasionally, it comes in the form of big, grand gestures, but its true power—internally and externally—exerts itself when you do it in small ways, consistently, every day. Kindness and good manners become your default, and if you practice them enough, they will.

So then why is this book called *Gracious* instead of *Manners*? Because while *manners* is a general term, *graciousness* implies the type of manners—and the outlook that supports and informs those manners—that I believe could maybe, possibly, perhaps rescue us from the ugliness of the modern world. Graciousness, which is only in part about manners and etiquette, has a moral core; place settings are but a tiny flourish on an enormous, architecturally sound whole. It's assigning and extending humanity to everyone you meet—creating beauty where you can, showing love even, and *especially*, when you don't feel like it. It's delighting in and celebrating the things that bring us, and others, joy. It is realizing that the small things, which may seem so trifling, can anchor us to our best selves. They can weave together to hold the ugliness at bay. It is knowing that all we want, at the end of the day, is to be recognized, to be welcomed kindly, to be made to feel comfortable in a life, which is, by definition, uncomfortable.

A lot of times, when someone does something sweet for us, a natural response is "Oh, you didn't have to do that!" And yeah, *of course,* they didn't have to do it; there is no state or federal law that requires bringing someone a muffin because you overheard them say they were hungry and you know they are at the end of their rope. There is no merit or virtue in the things we *have* to do; it's the things we *want* and *choose* to do that make the difference.

I will say, the one and only time I did mushrooms, I thought I'd solved the Problem of Humanity. Unfortunately, my solution to the void inside all of us was to smile beatifically and say, "You know what? We are all just *people* on the *planet.*" I did this in response to any question or comment, all evening. So, really, this is only a solution for someone who is currently on mushrooms.

At least compared to being in the womb. Can't speak for ghosts here, as I am not one.

Wait! Does Anyone Actually Do That?

Yes, many! When we find those people who give us that comfort, compassion, and love, we are drawn to them naturally. Luckily, they don't seem to mind because, by definition, they seem to be big fans of humanity.

Growing up, I had a lot of wonderful people modeling this brand of graciousness for me—Mrs. Scott, Mrs. Provosty, Miss Gabi, Miss Virginia, Mrs. Rigney, Miss Fumiko, Mrs. Rembrand, Miss Roz—if they were REALLY close family friends, you got to call them Miss Firstname, which was just *thrilling*. Even when I was a tiny little girl, you could just . . . tell that there was something special about them. They always seemed so confident and reassuring; they were solidly in themselves no matter the circumstances. They were always able to say something meaningful or funny at the right moment.

They moved slowly and deliberately. They paused before they spoke, so when they opened their mouths they said precisely what they meant. They had, and have, a way of appearing with the right card/baked good/paint rollers for whatever the situation required. I felt like the queen of England when I was in their houses. If I knocked over my glass of cranberry juice and sparkling water, which was garnished with a thin slice of lemon, they didn't yell or even seem particularly perturbed. Even though I was little, they had so many questions for me and would really engage with my answers, nodding in agreement as though I'd just said something quite profound about the plastic toy I'd asked Santa for. There was something about them that made me, and everyone in their orbit, feel so special and so loved.

I used to be a reporter at a daily newspaper (great, great career choice, 2004-era Kelly!), and one of my favorite jobs was writing the Sunday profile. I'd follow my subject around for at least a week, talking through their entire life and sometimes just watching them at work, doing whatever they did just because it made them happy

---

Other Southerners may disagree on this, but I find the pronunciation of "Ms.," "Mrs.," and "Miss" to be identical—Mizzz. Also, for some reason, first-name-only is styled as Miss Firstname, regardless of marital status.

or they felt it should be done. Because of this, a good subject was critical, both to engender a story that was worth the reader's investment and, selfishly, because I had to spend a LOT of time with this person and it would be a bummer to my editor if that time resulted in nothing to fill the hungry, hungry news hole.🍍

One profile search strategy always worked. I would call up one of my sources—the administrative assistant at city hall, or the office of the Oregon State Fair—and ask them, who is the most interesting and lovely person you know?

Then I would call that person—a winemaker or hairdresser or lady who drives around with a truck full of things for the homeless people in town, all of whom she knows by name—and ask if I could follow them around for a week.

Within 30 seconds of conversation, I could tell when I had a great subject on my hands. The first thing, *the very first thing*, that the truly fascinating people would say, nearly word for word, was: "Oh, I don't think you want to interview me. I am *so* boring. Have you thought about So-and-so?"

So-and-so is great, I would agree, but I was really, really hoping to interview them. Could they please just meet me for coffee?

They'd ask which coffee shop I liked and when would work for me. Occasionally they would be so, so sorry but they just can't possibly meet today because an immediate family member is actually getting a medical procedure in an hour. They might accidentally let it slip that the procedure in question is a quadruple bypass, but *nothing to worry about*, a minor logistical issue that I shouldn't trouble myself with. At this point I would usually start to wonder, Why on earth were they on the phone with me? Shouldn't they be storming around the house trying to push over heavy furniture? Weeping and rending their garments in the town square, cursing cruel Fortuna and

🍍 The news hole is the amount of copy–inches of story, which is literally the newspaper's unit of measurement–that is required to fill the paper. It depends on how many ads were sold and what day of the week it is and maybe Saturn's location. Many variables are in play. Anyway, my friends Nancy and Rachel called it the hungry, hungry news hole–gross, hilarious, and accurate.

her wheel? That's what I would do if anyone I know was getting his *appendix* removed, but then again, I am not very gracious.

Once we'd sit down for coffee, after they insisted on paying no matter how many times I said it was my treat, they wouldn't talk about themselves, and when they did, it was only after I'd ask point-blank questions that couldn't possibly be turned back toward me, which was what they *really* seemed to want to talk about.

They would say that it must be fascinating to be a reporter, and oh, I must see so many interesting things! Each day would be a fantastic new adventure! How glamorous! How perfectly fabulous that I'm a writer, a *professional writer*, Salem is so very lucky to have me, and they think my column is just a *hoot*. How am I liking Salem, which neighborhood do I live in, have I had the pleasure of meeting X, Y, and Z yet, oh I should, they would just *adore* me and they are all so fun and smart, do I miss New Orleans, do I have siblings, and if so how many and where do they live, WOW, San Francisco and Seattle, a reporter, a graphic designer, and an Xbox employee, our mom must be *so proud of us! * Gosh. That is just *wonderful.*

You might have read that paragraph and thought: Bullshit. That is not real, and if it is, it's not sincere. But I promise you, it was both to the core, which is one of the Deep and Abiding Mysteries of Gracious People. This could go on for hours, and I'm ashamed to say I fell for it the first few times. "Oh my God," I thought. "What a serendipitous meeting! I didn't know it, but apparently this person had been sitting around, *dying* to know what my life is like, and now I get to tell them! On company time! Wow!"

But what I gradually realized was that this quality of expressing a real interest in people that they were with and the ability to be fully present during their interactions was precisely why someone had nominated them to be interviewed in the first place.

Once I caught on to their tricks, I began developing techniques for gently asking questions and dragging out personal information from them. That's when I would find out that, yes, they did get their PhD in physics back when women were barely allowed in college, and as a matter of fact, it *was* they who single-handedly oversaw the Capitol renovation, and technically, they *do* throw an individual birthday party for every single person in the city every year, but they have so much help, you know? Besides, everyone loves a birthday party, and it's just no trouble at all to throw one.

What is the foundation that anchors your beautiful heart? I always wanted to ask. How did you become this way? How do I get from where I am to where you are? Is it possible for me to be a human who moves serenely and steadily through life, who has done astonishing things and yet has sufficient sense of self that she does not need the validation of others? How do you live a life where kindness and assurance, instead of anxiety and irritation, are the emotional guideposts? Where in yourself do you find that deep wellspring of ease and comfort that washes over everyone around you? Finally, is there room in your home for me to move in? Because logistically, financially, and emotionally I am on board.

There is an intoxication to the gracious people among us, a charisma that originates not from a perfect smile or any of the outside trappings of beauty, composure, or coordination. What I began to realize in the course of these interviews is that these gracious people moved through the world radiating an invisible but beautiful space of compassion and caring, one that they are happy to share with any human who wants to be a part of it. As Emily Post wrote in the very first edition of *Etiquette:*

> *Best Society is not a fellowship of the wealthy . . . it is an association of gentle-folk, of which good form in speech, charm of manner, knowledge of the social amenities, and instinctive consideration for the feelings of others are the credentials.*

In writing this book, I wanted to find this Best Society, to ask those who are a part of it how they do it. I wanted to find a way to do it myself, or at least come close, and to share their thoughts and advice with you and the rest of the world.

To find my interview subjects for this book, I did the same thing that I did back when trying to find a Sunday profile subject—I talked to everyone, describing the kind of woman I was thinking of: the brilliant conversationalist, the fascinating hostess, the elegantly dressed septuagenarian who cracks dirty jokes when it's just she and her friends—a North Star, orienting you toward what you want to be. When I was searching for interview subjects for this book, people would light up when I told them what kind of person I was looking for. "I KNOW EXACTLY WHO YOU'RE TALKING ABOUT!" they'd say. "You know, so, the . . . okay, this is complicated, but the mother of my ex-boyfriend from high school. I don't talk to him anymore, he was kind of an asshole and that was 15 years ago, but I LOVE his mother, and we keep in touch on Facebook. I'll ask her if I can give you her number."

And then I would call that woman and ask if I could talk to her. She would laugh when I told her what the book was about, then she'd ask if I was sure if I wanted to interview her? I was absolutely, positively, 1,000 percent sure.

That is how you, gracious reader, came to be holding this little book. Graciousness is everywhere; it knows no class, culture, or domestic requirement. It is not about hosting a perfect party or dressing in a certain way (although we'll talk about how to alleviate any anxieties you may have in either of those areas). Graciousness is about finding a way to be comfortable in your own skin, and then using that security to make others feel comfortable, too. It is an outlook leading to actions that lets you feel good about the day or at least your actions in it. Graciousness is about facing the world with kindness and compassion rather than with ambivalence or just suspicion.

I hope you adore these women and their brilliant insights as much as I do. I hope you find some things very useful and other things, if not so useful, then perhaps at least funny. I hope this book gives you a small bit of the happiness and warm feelings that come when you're in the physical presence of graciousness. Most importantly, I hope that you recognize and, if you want, cultivate your own wonderful qualities and abilities and that you celebrate the astonishing wealth of interesting and lovely people, places, and things around us. It can be hard to train yourself to notice, but it is in that noticing that we will all make the world a more gracious place, one moment at a time.

Now, if you'll go ahead and turn the page, I'd be very grateful. There are some absolutely wonderful human beings ahead who you'll probably just *adore*.

CHAPTER ONE

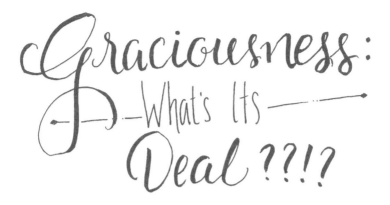

Graciousness: What's Its Deal ??!?

Dear reader,

Hello! Welcome to the first chapter!

Because the word *gracious* evokes so many things, I decided that perhaps a (metaphorical, y'all) trip way, way back in time was in order to get us all on the same page. We are, in fact, going back to the beginning of people talking to each other. If you would, please, hop into this well-appointed, comfortable yet stylish Imagination Machine, and off we go!

Grace is a word that stretches back to the beginning of words, first appearing pre-Sanskrit as *gwreto*, "to favor." Between then and now, grace and its variations have spread through space and time. It appeared as three goddesses in ancient Greek with the Charites, who oversaw the intersection of charm, art, and beauty, which, in turn, they gave freely to others.

Grace applies to all sorts of things—how you move through the world physically, socially, emotionally—but it almost always implies performing whatever you're doing well and seemingly effortlessly. Also, according to the Greeks, it includes "adornment, mirth, festivity, dance, and song" plus "the other pleasures of life,

---

Hopefully it goes without saying that our Imagination Machine has a vast number of upholstered chaise longues, flattering lighting, cuddly Maine coons and/or pugs, crafting supplies for if we get bored, and rosé.

including play, amusement, banqueting, floral decoration, happiness, rest, and relaxation," which I am fairly sure we can agree is an inclusive list of what makes life worth living. UP WITH BANQUETING, REST, RELAXATION, AND AMUSEMENT!

It's also spawned words like *gratitude, charisma, charity,* and *gratify.*

It's a word that is both feminine and divine, unlike most ancient feminine words, which often seem to be something along the lines of root vegetable/soil/something to put a penis into, etc.

The reason that we have these words, still, and in so many languages, is that they express something universal, something we feel that is huge and hard to sum up.

It may, in fact, be easier to start with what graciousness is not:

🌸 Graciousness has nothing to do with being born with a certain amount of money or in a certain place or at a certain time. It does not know ethnicity, gender, class, place, or any other born-with quality you can name. It is free. It is available to everyone, anytime.

🌸 A gracious person is not a doormat. If you are imagining someone who exists solely as a social Santa Claus, showing up and giving everyone what they want, stop right there. I mean, gracious people DO do that second one, but they do so as a by-product of the strong sense of who they are, what they want, and how they live life.

🌸 Graciousness is not an inherent trait, like your shoe size or eye color. It is a skill, and like every other skill in the world, you have to work at it. This may sound like a tall order, but it's actually not. It is, in fact, relatively easy, does not require enormous amounts of energy or resources, and is completely worth it, plus you get to try it any old time!

Merriam-Webster defines graciousness, in part, as marked by kindness and courtesy; marked by tact and delicacy; urbane; characterized by charm, good taste, and generosity of spirit.

I don't know about you, but I want all of those things in my life, every day.

I want to be the person who knows just what to say when someone is being awful and needs to be called out—perhaps even with a whispered "Shame on you!"—but also recognizes that this is a human being who deserves to be treated humanely. I want to feel comfortable gliding through scary social situations ranging from walking into a party by myself to hosting a big event. I want to be able to make friends wherever I go; to welcome guests graciously to my house and never, ever let them see me sweat. I want to feel at ease whether I'm talking to hog farmers or Savannah society. I want to defend my ideas and my freedom of speech in a way that leads to understanding rather than Twitter catfights.

"Graciousness, to me, conjures up being thoughtful, being kind, being considerate, thinking before you act or speak—in other words, thinking about whomever you're with and not being so focused on you," said Dorothy Buckhanan Wilson. "It's making sure that *whomever* you are interacting with leaves that interaction feeling a sense of dignity and self-worth . . . it's not about making an impression as much as it is thinking to yourself, what can you do to make their day a little bit better?"

Dorothy then gave me something so beautiful. She said that as she moves through life, she tries hard to always deposit something positive, something kind, something uplifting, something helpful in her wake. I imagined a map of the world, a golden line tracing her paths and small, glittering gems that she's scattered everywhere she goes. Then I paused for a moment and wondered what my map would look like, whether I was leaving something lovely, something unremarkable, or something ugly. And I can own the answer: It's a mix of all three, and sometimes more of that last one than I'm comfortable with.

You know, Ms. Buckhanan Wilson—and every person I quote in this book—deserves a full introduction so you know her. It is, however, hard to do a proper introduction without totally interrupting her brilliant words, but if you'll flip to page 110, you can get to know her a bit better. Trust me, you want to, because she is an *amazing woman*.

I am capable of impressive ungracious acts. (Brief example: Just today, my best friend was telling me about her very painful breakup, and I interrupted her to reference a completely unrelated YouTube video. WHY DID I DO THAT?!)

We all do and say things we regret—rushing through life with our head down, rarely giving the present moment—and people— the thought and care they deserve. That kind of attention is rare enough that when you are with someone gracious, you *know* it. Or, more accurately, you feel it. You feel smarter, kinder, more loving, more capable. That is the gift that a gracious person gives to you and to everyone—which is why it's a universally sought-after quality.

Despite all this evidence of the inherent goodness of graciousness, people talk as though it's gone or at least is going extinct.

"Oh my gosh, wouldn't it be *amazing* if people still had manners?" I've heard many people say, gazing out a rain-streaked window as if searching for that Polite Brigadoon, forever lost to the ages and perhaps only a myth, but oh, such a beautiful story!

Younger people (and older ones, too!) sometimes act as though graciousness, tact, and civility are rare earth minerals, the last of which were mined in 1977. Or, alternately, that a return to manners would mean the end of freedom and progress—that by embracing this aspect of the past, we also condone and invite in all the atrocious, racist, sexist, homophobic, intolerant awfulness of that time period. (All those things, of course, still exist. For more on how to respond to and rise above them and how you can be on the right side of things, see Chapter 3, Grace Under Fire.)

Graciousness is, however, a little bit endangered. We live in a time when it's so easy to be rude, so easy to always think about ourselves first. We spend a lot of time talking about ourselves at each other, and not as much time listening. It is very hard to focus on doing anything, let alone cultivating graciousness, well, when there are about 50 other things that required your attention yesterday. Things move very, very fast, and the pace of life can leave us working so hard to keep up that we forget about the basic humanity of those working equally hard around us.

But I have learned that graciousness is a skill that anybody can develop—like all skills, you develop it by practice—despite how quickly our individual worlds are spinning on any given day. You can do it, right now, today. Or at least you can start having it or continue to have it or tend to it like a delicate but withered orchid. If you'd like to! Obviously, no one can or will make you, but I would argue it's worth a go.

You should *want* to be gracious for virtuous and noble reasons, and I'm sure you do! However, it certainly doesn't hurt that there are many . . . let's say *tangible* and *immediate* payoffs. To name a few . . .

- People will want to be around you. Crass Accounting of Payoffs (CAPs): more friends, more social opportunities, more laser tag/boating/etc. invitations!

- A sense of personal integrity and comfort within your own skin. CAPs: better sleep, less anxiety and fretting, an ability to let small things go!

- You will be shocked—*shocked*, I tell you!—by how much of it will be reflected right back at you, by how kind other humans are when they are given the slightest opportunity or opening. CAPs: the ability to get customer service to actually help you, the satisfaction of knowing you made someone else's day better, and sometimes, free stuff from the convenience store.

- Being . . . well . . . if not waterproof, then at least water-*resistant* to the sadness/meanness of those around you. You will become submergible, up to 30 meters, and emerge intact and unchanged. CAPs: not feeling personally hurt every time someone doesn't treat you exactly the way you'd like to be treated; the smug satisfaction that comes with being able to

(continued on page 8)

MEET Miss Leslie & THE POCKET MANUAL of REPUBLICAN Etiquette

When I began researching this book, I had *no idea* of the glorious bounty of old, copyright-expired etiquette books that were in my immediate future! After downloading 17 of them and printing out my 6 favorites, 2 clear winners stood out.

The first—written by Samuel R. Wells in 1857—*could* have gotten in on title alone—that title being . . . ready for this?

How to Behave: A Pocket Manual of Republican Etiquette and Guide to Correct Personal Habits,

Embracing an Exposition of the Principles of Good Manners; Useful Hints on the Care of the Person, Eating, Drinking, Exercise, Habits, Dress, Self-Culture, and Behavior at Home; the Etiquette of Salutations, Introductions, Receptions, Visits, Dinners, Evening Parties, Conversation, Letters, Presents, Weddings, Funerals, the Street, the Church, Places of Amusement, Traveling, Etc.,

With Illustrative Anecdotes, a Chapter on Love and Courtship, and Rules of Order for Debating Societies

The second and the *clear* standout was from 1839, and its title is just as good:

Miss Leslie's Behaviour Book; A Guide and Manual for Ladies,

As Regards Their Conversation; Manners; Dress; Introductions; Entrée to Society; Shopping; Conduct in the Street at Places of Amusement, in Traveling, at the Table, Either at Home, in Company, or at Hotels; Deportment in Gentlemen's Society; Lips; Complexion; Teeth; Hands; the Hair; Etc., Etc.

With Full Instructions and Advice in

Letter Writing; Receiving Presents; Incorrect Words; Borrowing; Obligations to Gentlemen; Offenses; Children; Decorum in Church, at

Evening Parties; and Suggestions in Bad Practices and Habits Easily Contracted, Which No Young Lady Should Be Guilty of, Etc., Etc.

—◦◇◦—

Miss Leslie is *wonderful*—fabulously Jane Austen-ish, Mean Girl-esque, when the time is right. If she lived now, she would be a beloved Internet writer. Much of what she said is delightful, and I will be peppering her quotes, along with those from the *Pocket Manual of Republican Etiquette,* throughout this book.

These books were *clearly* written for self-conscious rich white people, trying to make sure that the other rich white people thought well of them, and some of the details are astonishing—who knew you could go on for *12 damn pages* about when to put on or take off your gloves?

But! It was striking how many of the principles of kindness, compassion, and giving comfort to others are just as clear and relevant as can be.

In fact, it's almost disarming, because you'll be reading and *really* getting into it and then suddenly Miss Leslie will drop a bomb like this on you:

On no consideration question the servants, or talk to them about the family, *particularly* if they are slaves.

. . . and you have *never* felt more grateful for progress and the passage of time, because, oh my God, slavery was just off-handedly mentioned as one more etiquette principle? Like, the ownership of humans? By other humans? Just, make sure not to be rude to the humans who are hosting you and not pestering the *humans they own* for details about their lives? Because it would call their loyalty to their employer/OWNER into question? *WHAT?*

The 1800s, ladies and gentlemen! Definitely not as long ago as we'd like.

think, 'Oh well! Sorry you feel and behave that way!' and move on mentally.

If you are on board, here is how you begin.

You must know—really and truly believe, reminding yourself again and again, every day—that every human on earth is just as human as you are.

Sure, we all know this, and yet it can immediately slip from our minds. It is all too easy to get trapped in our own heads, treating our own mental and emotional sludge as though it is a real thing in the world, a filter through which we judge or ignore everything around us. Meanwhile, everyone else is doing the same damn thing!

It is not our natural state to feel the humanity of those around us, to let it sink into our bones, to recognize it as a fact of nature that is just as real, powerful, and omnipresent as gravity.

Once, in college, I asked my astronomy professor if it ever bothered him how big space was, how small we are, how anything could happen randomly. His class made me horrifically anxious; I spent a *lot* of time worrying about the sun and whether or not it would choose the next day to explode and end all life and everything I knew. I shared this fear with him, hoping for some sympathy.

No, he said. No, it didn't bother him, because everywhere you go, the laws of physics remain the same (except for certain circumstances, but I will end this recollection here because I have no idea what he said but am pretty sure it had something to do with black holes and quarks).

"True politeness is perfect freedom and ease, treating others just as you love to be treated."

—A Pocket Manual of Republican Etiquette (PMRE) makes the Golden Rule sound so exquisitely decadent

My point is, though, that the laws of graciousness are just as consistent and constant as the laws of physics; yes, there are probably some exceptions, but you'll be a lot less stressed if you assume that they're true until a specific situation proves otherwise. And one of those laws is recognizing the humanity of whoever is next to you at that moment.

Unless you are a lonely groundskeeper, your only companion a loyal and quiet hedgehog, or midway through a solo boat trip around the world (if so, bon voyage! Please observe best practices for nautical safety! Thank you for making the odd choice to bring *this* book along!), nearly every morning, afternoon, and evening will contain encounters with the following:

- People whom you love with all your heart who never, ever disappoint you, let you down, or behave in any way other than the Platonic ideal of [spouse/friend/coworker/convenience store employee🍍]: 0.1 percent

- People whom you love with all your heart who *do* let you down, sometimes: 12.4 percent

- People whom you sometimes love, sometimes like, sometimes . . . well, sometimes other: 12.5 percent

- Indifferent people, those who are sitting at the other table in the café or in the car ahead of you on the highway, or perhaps just that coworker with whom a tepid acknowledgment is mutual: 78.7 percent

- Unfriendly people: 6.2 percent🍍🍍

We wade through our days sometimes feeling a bit affronted by all these other humans, who are not us, who do not share our precise mood and concerns and joys at that moment, who want or need things from us, who adore us or hate our guts, or who have their own agendas and history and blood sugar levels.

This would be galling enough, but it goes a step further: To

(continued on page 14)

🍍 This actually does exist. Hi, Keith!

🍍🍍 Though it's easy to inflate this figure, it is, in fact, 6.2 percent of humanity that is acting in bad faith at any given moment. Usually, what we think unfriendly is actually indifferent, which is to say, they don't think a thing about you except that you are between them and the door they are trying to walk through.

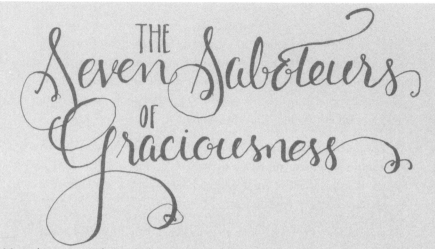

THE Seven Saboteurs OF Graciousness

Most things, people, and places in this life are well intentioned, even if their wonderfulness is not immediately apparent. Most people, as my Grannybarb would say, are doing their best, even though some people's best is pretty shitty.

The vast majority of the time, people respond to kindness and consideration in kind. But sometimes they don't. Sometimes they say something mean or do something that hurts, *and we will never know why.* Nor do we need to! Correcting the behavior of others, unless they are a minor child under our guardianship, is not gracious (or useful).

The behavior we can hope to have any influence over is our own. No one else's is up to us, and even if it was, they wouldn't listen anyway, so let's not worry about it.

But we do need to react to other people's behavior, even when that behavior is perhaps less than perfect. We get to decide what we bring to that interaction, and hopefully we decide to bring our best.

So here, now, are the Seven Saboteurs of Graciousness,※ which represent actions and motivations that try to strike against graciousness. You'll find them throughout the book, popping in to say or do things that we should view as *exciting opportunities to hone our own graciousness* instead of just terrible behavior.

You will surely recognize them from real life in others and, unfortunately, in yourself.

※ Originally, they were going to have alliterative names, like Inconsiderate Casey. But then I thought about any Caseys who might read this book feeling increasingly annoyed as their namesake behaved badly again and again, in exactly the same way. It wouldn't be right.

The  Self-Absorbed

Seems to process all information in terms of how it relates to or affects them, ignoring completely that which doesn't. Things, situations, and people are all assessed based on how they help, hurt, or validate this all-important, endlessly fascinating self. This can also manifest as self-loathing, which is just the flip side of our little narcissist coin.

Classic Self-Absorbed: Interrupts you while you are crying to muse about how your painful breakup actually made them question their relationship but it's such a different story and actually Kyle is the perfect person for them and what do you think, just theoretically, of fall weddings?

THE Combative

Always so very, very ready to take things seven notches above what the situation calls for. This may be temper, or it may be the need to play devil's advocate to the point where it becomes an excuse to say things that they know will hurt others under cover of "exploring every angle." May be heard complaining bitterly about how So-and-so and those people and this place and that group are out to get them.

Classic Combative: Picking a political fight on a nonpolitical Facebook post with someone they don't know.

THE Thoughtless

Prone to speaking or acting before they think and equally prone to saying something off-color or hurtful. It never occurred to them that you might take their remark seriously or consider it for more than a nanosecond—they sure didn't! They meant nothing by it! If their attention is drawn to this, they feel genuinely terrible. They feel genuinely terrible very, very frequently.

Classic Thoughtless: Even though they RSVP'd yes to your dinner party, they call an hour ahead of time to say that they're feeling sad and blah and won't be attending or bringing that dessert they offered to make.

THE *Crude*

Purposefully says or does things that *are completely inappropriate to the situation* and, as a result, makes everyone feel ill at ease. This can range from the very mild (using salty language in a place where salty language is not welcome) to the truly monstrous (using power to demean and dehumanize people; purposefully making someone feel afraid). Sometimes, they mean nothing by it and perhaps have no idea what they're doing. The worst of the Crudes, however, know exactly what they're doing.

Classic Crude: Thinks a rape joke is funny and just the thing to liven up this Girls Inc. fund-raiser.

THE *Meddler*

Has so, *so many* thoughts and suggestions about what you should do or what your sick friend should do or what someone has done that is *totally unacceptable* according to their layered and nuanced algorithms, deployed constantly for their important work of judging others. The Meddler also tends to blend in the opinions of others with their own, even if those opinions were shared in confidence and are hurtful. Unlike the Thoughtless, whose crimes are passive and unintentional, the Meddler sets about their business with *purpose* and *zeal.*

Classic Meddler: Offers unsolicited advice about your relationship, which is to end it, and then notes that they are not the only one who feels this way.

THE *Resentful*

The pains and insults of the past, plus the Ghost of Suffering Yet to Come, all form a very dark lens through which the world is viewed. Happiness is a zero-sum game; someone else's joy means there is less available for them (not that there was much to begin with). Comparison is the thief of joy, and the Resentful never, ever stops keeping score.

Classic Resentful: Smiles briefly and tightly when you tell them you got the job you were dreaming of, then says, "Oh, great. That's so great for you. Congratulations. It's so nice that things always just go so well for you."

THE Enigma

Who knows, man? Who could even begin to fathom a guess of what they meant by saying or doing whatever they just said or did? Life is full of mysteries, and the Enigma is constantly adding to this compendium by saying or doing something that strikes the rest of us as just plain *batshit crazy*.

Classic Enigma: Response to a question about how their day is going includes one of the following: human breast milk and its culinary possibilities; the Illuminati; a thought that begins "So I figured out what we need to do about . . . " and ends with a racial slur.

If, when reading, you found one of the descriptions hits a little too close to home, well, *of course it does!* We all behave in these ways—in fact, I'm guessing that not a day goes by when I don't embody each of the Saboteurs at some point.

We are all but cranky, imperfect little meat bundles with skeletons inside, wandering around and trying to do our best, so if and when you are being the gracious challenge, that's okay. Just pause, notice, and then ask yourself why you are doing this—a good first step is to run through the Am I Hungry? Angry? Lonely? Tired? checklist.

If you find that there is one behavior in others that drives you up the wall, well . . . just remember that we tend to get most angry when we see our own defects reflected back to us.

"Good manners and good morals are founded on the same eternal principles of right and are only different expressions of the same great truths. Both grow out of the necessities of our existence and relations. We have individual rights based on the fact of our individual being; and we have social duties resulting from our connection, in the bonds of society, with other individuals who have similar rights."

—The *PMRE* distills the moral essence of good manners down to perfection.

accomplish nearly anything, we need them. We rely constantly not only on the person next to us but also on enormous systems of humanity that are both invisible and infinitely more complicated than we'd have ever imagined.

Every moment! I'm not kidding! Examine the most banal moment of your day—let's say, for example, asking a librarian the location of a book that you *don't* want but is probably close to the book you *do* want but are embarrassed to request.

Here is 0.01 percent of what happened before that moment that allows you to ask for this book:

1. The librarian in question dedicated nearly a decade to scholarly pursuits, getting first a bachelor's and then master's degree in English, literature, and/or library science, relying on thousands of years of human knowledge, dozens of professors who dedicated *their* lives to the same study, and the Dewey decimal system, to prepare him or her to answer your question, and who also is the product of every human who, as Mr. Rogers said, loved them into being.

2. Before that, *another* librarian looked at this book that you

Live the FABULOUS Skinny Gurl Life of Your Dreams, as Interpreted by Love Interests from Novels about Vampires and People Who Have a Loose Understanding of BDSM and Also One of the Real Housewives Is on the Cover, While Getting the Compliments You DESERVE! Part IV

want and thought, "Ah! That seems like something we should have!" and then bought it, and no one has stolen it since.

3. One *more* librarian (spoiler: It's all librarians! Just layers upon layers of them! *Librarians all the way down!*) cut little pieces of paper for you to write your book number on before you walked (on carpet that someone installed) to the computer (that someone else set up) to talk with the first librarian who made his or her way to work using public or private transit that likely involved interacting with dozens of other people on their way to work who were not rushing quite as fast as to cause any kind of delays.

[Edited for space: a very *rich* and *moving* narrative sweep that included, but was not limited to, the terrifying and sudden nature of tornadoes, production of the internal combustion engine, what life aboard an off-shore oil rig is like, an amusing discourse on why golf pencils are the best and worst and how none of us, when you think about it, is actually able to make a pencil, all the people who were on the bus with you, etc., etc., etc., etc., on an infinite loop. Technically, it is not just librarians all the way down. It's humans all the way down.]

The point of this thought exercise is to take a moment to appreciate just how many people had to take a certain kind of action in order to facilitate every single thing that happens to you all day. Think of all the people involved in the creation and maintenance of the library (and of the roads that lead to the library, and so on) to all of the people who work to ensure that the food, shelter, transportation, electricity, and other resources you use every day are available. To be gracious—which is awfully close to grateful—is to live in a way that acknowledges all these extremely convenient miracles that allow you to get the books, products, and services that you desire. No matter what else is going on in your life, you will find yourself a lot happier and less stressed out if you take a few moments every day to remember how many things had to go right in order for you to get that cup of coffee that took a few more minutes than you wish it had.

Think IN TERMS OF "*Us*"

I once read that in a marriage, you should try to always think in terms of "us," and that you can tell a marriage is over when the couple isn't thinking in "us" terms anymore, but rather as a you and a me who have different, competing objectives. You get your way, then I get my way, or maybe you always get your way, etc.

The "us" framework treats both parties as a unit—yes, their interests may be different or even in conflict, but the central question is what action moves that "us" forward?

Try thinking about *every* relationship, no matter how brief, as an "us." It doesn't matter if that "us" is you and your spouse or you and the person behind the rental car counter. For however long or short a time that interaction may last, there *is* an "us."

What action, on your end, helps the "us" in the rental car counter example meet both your need to get a car and their need to do their job competently?

This is a very gracious position: You are neither people-pleasing, which entirely takes *you* out of the picture and is bound to leave you feeling unsatisfied, nor are you thinking just about what *you* want in this given moment regardless of how that impacts the person on the other end of the transaction.

You and Not-You are, in these minutes or months or decades, on the same team. Act accordingly.

Tens or hundreds of times per day, we interact with others. Over a lifetime, this number likely runs into the millions and forms not only the majority of what we will do on this earth but also what that earth is like. Or at least, what our little corner of it is like. We decide, every moment, who we shall be and what we are going to add into the world with our words and actions or lack thereof.

Take this to the bank, dear ones, and please deposit it quickly:

Though your time with Others may be at most temporary, no one is disposable or discardable, the human equivalent of a golf pencil. To treat people otherwise dishonors not only them but also this entire neat system that we live in, in which we depend on one another in ways both tiny and unimaginably huge. It dishonors the heart of what you, and what all of us, tend to want: to be treated as though we matter, with civility.

> "Good manners are not to be put on and off with one's best clothes. Politeness is an article for everyday wear. If you don it only on special and rare occasions, it will be sure to sit awkwardly upon you."
>
> —The *PMRE*, on consistency

The universe, as we all know and as is demonstrated daily by my kitchen sink, is constantly trending toward chaos and entropy. But no matter how chaotic it is, we can be peaceful in the middle of that if we know what is and what is not up to us.

We are not asked for input on whether that embarrassing book is in stock or if that librarian is in a sour mood due to an impending divorce or if a freak tornado is going to hit the library 17 minutes from now. We *can* decide the quality of our side of that interaction. It is, really, the only shot we get to call every time.

If you can remember this, at least sometimes, you will be gracious. When you approach each person and situation without expectations or entitlement, but rather just with the principles that you want to live by, then whatever you get back is just fine with you. If you can momentarily pause your annoyance or frustration, take a deep breath, and figure out the right thing for you to do in this moment, well, congratulations! That's graciousness in a nutshell.

To be gracious is to bring ease and comfort into a world that is anything but easy or comfortable, and you feel that ease most acutely within your own skin.

This is the only indisputable fact in the book; from here on out, it's all opinions, conjecture, and argument.

> "Accustom yourself to a sacred regard for the rights of others, even in the minutest matters, and in the most familiar intercourse of the family or social circle."
>
> —The *PMRE*, on being sweet to your mamma

If you are reading this and saying, *Yes, yes, that's all well and good—shall I also walk on water? Discover my own Buddha nature and find perfect contentment in the Now of the DMV? Turn packing peanuts into a beautiful fleet of immortal butterflies that can live happily in my apartment forever? What other enormous, impossible things will be asked of me before this chapter is over?* I don't blame you. It does sound like a lot.

But you would never feel bad about, say, not knowing how to weld if you've never learned a thing about welding. Same deal with being gracious. Think of yourself as an apprentice welder, on the verge of jumping into the amazing, satisfying, and profitable world of attaching one bit of metal to another bit of metal. Except you are going to be welding love and friendship and overall kindness and decency. You are a welder of great conversations, of lifelong friendships, of being able to express what you need to say without fear of offense.

In the coming pages, you'll hear about how to deal with all manners of social traps, snares, and bedevilments; you'll master the art of good conversation; you'll be able to be at home wherever you go. People refer to these as "soft skills," which is so diminishing, so ignorant of the power of these gifts. We may as well call them "tiny puff skills."

Take, for example, my friend Nora. Nora is someone whom it would be so very easy to resent, because she looks like a Disney princess–spring fairy hybrid, with naturally blonde hair and more happiness than seems humanly possible. Often during a conversation, Nora is so happy for you that she JUST *CAN'T BELIEVE* IT! This declaration is accompanied with an enormous smile, mouth slightly open, shaking her head in amazement. A very short, non-comprehensive list of things that Nora has not been able to believe (at least during our friendship):

- The fact that homemade toffee is available to eat

- The wonders of a SodaStream

- A holiday wreath I hot-glued together out of dollar-store orna-
ments, because it *looks like a professional made it!*

- That we are both enjoying a particularly tasty pork dish

- The fact that I was going to be in Los Angeles for a few days

One might read this and think Nora is insincere or even a teeny
bit ditzy. You would be *profoundly wrong on every count* (and also
I would smack you in the face for thinking such things. I'm dead
serious, even though I know slapping sense into people is the opposite of gracious and has no place in our modern, slap-free society,
plus slapping someone on her behalf would appall Nora).

She is exceedingly thoughtful, the kind of person who will invite
you over for "a light snack" that will include not one but three
delightful courses of light food—savory, savory, *and* sweet!

Nora's joy and optimism come from a place of humility and
wonder. Yes, she is genuinely that happy for you! She is dying—she
may *literally* expire—to hear all about your life when you sit down
with her. And here is why. For Nora, there is nothing more interesting in the world than other people. In fact, the very idea of thinking
about one's self all the time strikes her as profoundly boring.

"If you thought constantly about yourself, I think you might
not be a very interesting person," she told me. "Think about how
many people you know—hundreds? Thousands? Wouldn't life

"We have rights as well as you, one of which is to
exclude from our circle all persons whose manners or habits
are distasteful to us. You talk of rights. You cannot blame
others for exercising theirs."

—The *PMRE*, on why people who make rape jokes cannot
claim First Amendment protection

Theories of Grace

Readers! There is only one downside to getting to interview dozens of super-human humans, and that is when you are going through for quotes, you end up highlighting *everything*. Then, when trying to integrate every brilliant thing they said into a certain place in the book, you realize that it's too *good* to be sandwiched in and deserves its own space. So this is the first of several Theories of Grace that you'll find throughout the book. I want to let these amazing people speak in their own words; they are edited for length and in some cases rearranged for clarity.

Rabbi Rami M. Shapiro was the founding rabbi of Temple Beth Or and senior rabbi of Metivta, a center for contemplative Judaism in Los Angeles. He has written award-winning poetry and more than 30 beautiful books, including *Amazing Chesed: Living a Grace-Filled Judaism*.

I talked to him from his office in Miami, and when I asked him about his own theories of graciousness, here's what he said.

The actual word for "grace" in Hebrew is chen. Chesed *is more like compassion or loving-kindness, and they go together.*

If you understand God as existence itself, then grace is bestowed equally upon everyone. It's simply reality, and it's not always pleasant.

If you're hung up on judgment, then you're stuck in the binary of "I like this; I don't like that." I think that results in a tightening of the body and the breath and therefore the mind and the heart, and you find yourself incapable of moving graciously through any of it.

[When someone says something awful], my feeling in the moment is that's the only thing they could say. People are all trapped. My

spent thinking about hundreds or thousands of people be a lot more interesting than just one?"

Nora is always looking outward with positivity and good faith, and as a result, she is always delighted by what she sees. The land-

encounters with other people are, in a sense, outside anybody's control. People just say stuff because they're conditioned to say it, they're afraid, or they're trapped, so they lash out. None of that is premeditated or really deliberate on their part. I imagine most of what we do is simply preprogrammed.

It's realizing that everyone is trapped in her or his worldview, and once you know that, then compassion is the only response that makes sense. But compassion does not always equal presence. Even though I can have compassion toward your being trapped, I don't have to stick around and deal with it. I don't have to be your friend; I don't have to be your spouse.

I never think of [life] as imperfect or flawed, I think of it as just reality. Some things I like and some things I don't.

From a Jewish perspective, the world is the only way the world can be. It has to have good and bad and light and dark the same way that it has to have up and down.

It's the free gifting of the moment, and sometime those moments are wonderful and sometimes they're harrowing.

It's realizing that everything that happens to us is this effervescent flowing of divine reality and some of it we label as good and some of it we label as bad, but we have to accept all of it with what I would term "radical hospitality."

Radical hospitality is the acceptance of whatever's happening—thoughts, feelings, sensations, behaviors—of whatever's around us without resisting. You simply accept without any hesitation whatever is happening to you.

When you do that, you discover that you have the capacity to navigate whatever is happening graciously.

scape of her life is not one in which she is constantly berating herself or others. It is one with infinite possibility. Because she does not spend endless amount of time worrying about what other people think of her, she has time to actually do the things that others admire.

Virginia Provosty🍍—another star of a woman, whom you will hear much more from later—goes through her day in a similar manner.

"The most important thing," she said, "is to be present to what your job is here. Nowadays, it seems like we all run around, and we measure the success of our day by how breathless we get. We're bouncing off of each other like we're bumper cars, and we act like it doesn't hurt when we crash into each other.

"But the most valuable thing in the world is the human standing next to you. They're the gift. It's not the house, it's not the job, it's not the talent, it's not the beauty; it's the people next to you.

"When we blow people off and get into a hurry, which we all do because the world we live in *makes* us do that sometimes, we might miss the most important piece of the puzzle that we were looking for. People have lost the sense of mystery and wonder and connectedness to who they—who we—are.

"Capacity is what you're trying to increase in your life. Your capacity, your abilities to be compassionate and to love. So if you disengage from every uncomfortable person or situation in your life, you have lost that chance.

"Everybody needs the same thing, really, which is funny—we all need to be affirmed, to be listened to."

Virginia and Nora have hit upon the basic foundation of graciousness: gratitude, attention, and caring for other people.

"Once you begin honoring the people next to you and the time you have with them," Virginia said, "you *will* be a gracious person."

🍍 *Virginia is a landscape architect who grows all sorts of beautiful things outside New Orleans. She has known me since before I was born—she was pregnant with her first son, Townsend, at the same time my mom was pregnant with me.*

CHAPTER TWO

VIRTUALLY
Gracious

Since I began this book bemoaning those damned screens and their effects on the way we view ourselves and others, it seems natural to begin the conversation on how, exactly, we should treat those screens and how we should allow them to treat us.

Find your nearest chaise longue or fainting furniture of choice, for I have some very shocking news that may require many hours of physical and spiritual recuperation. The Internet Is Here to Stay, Forever (unless There Is Some Sort of Horrific Apocalypse).

The Internet offers, for better or often worse, a new dimension to how, where, and why humans can be wonderful and dreadful to each other.

Not only is it here to stay, but the Internet has gone right ahead and changed almost everything about how human beings (including elected national leaders!) interact. We do not have days to react to a letter; we have 10 minutes to reply to a text before rumors of our death begin circulating. We feel obligated to type out birthday wishes to someone we met at a house party 8 years ago, but we fail to reach out to friends *meaningfully* because we can keep vicarious tabs on them through what they choose to post on the Internet.

We carry around magical rectangles that can tell us anything that humans have ever said, thought, or did, and we have every reason to expect near-instant gratification. It's a blessing and a curse and can make us . . . a little rude.

Graciousness is about focused attention, kindness, and empathy and about moving deliberately in accordance with your values. The Internet is none of those things. It's a screaming toddler, except that we *need* this toddler. It's only been two (three?) decades, but now the idea of living without the Internet feels like living without opposable thumbs. We probably could, but oooooooh, that sounds like the biggest pain.

It gives us so much whenever we want it. It loves us. It hates us. It tells us how to get where we're going; it tells us that we will never get there. It is, in short, a perfect addiction, and we all could probably use a little less of it.

Or, at least, we could use less of the parts that take time away from what we are actually here to do. Those parts include, but are not limited to, wallowing in the hateful opinions of anonymous strangers, comparing everyone's outsides with your insides, getting in fights with people we have *never even seen, let alone talked to,* and encouraging you to live a life that looks great on paper—or in this case, pixels.

And we can keep it so close to us, because now the Internet fits in our purse! We keep it closer than our best friend, closer than our toothbrush, closer than our beloved dog. We buy adorable cases to protect it from falls, mobile hot spots to ensure good coverage, and car chargers so that we may never be without its company. It is always at hand, and it always has something to say.

"See?!" it seems to shriek, in its clattery, needy robot voice. "Everyone is racist! Everyone is awful! Oh, and hey—that person who was mean to you in middle school that you hate-friended on Facebook—she just went on a trip, with her husband, to Rome. Do you want to see? Hey, what about that dude who bullied you in seventh grade, whatshisname? MARIO! Ugh. He used to try to hit you in the face purposely with the volleyball during gym class, and

Coach Fischer always complimented him on his hustle? How's *he* doing? How are YOU doing? No, I mean, not how are you *actually* doing, but how great does the *world at large* think you're doing? Maybe you should just go ahead and spend the next 45 minutes artfully arranging a corner of your home and then another 15 minutes workshopping phrases that will make everyone, including that one ex, realize how perfect and wonderful YOU are? Are they thinking about YOU? They should be. Oh, good, a Like. Another one! 7, 8, 9! But why isn't it *15*?"

"Tattlers are always listeners and are frequently the atrocious writers of anonymous letters, for which they should be expelled from society."

—Miss Leslie is not even worked up about trolls.

I don't mean to sound pessimistic; the Internet is a beautiful and astonishing tool that has changed almost every facet of human existence. The Internet lets people who might otherwise have felt completely alone in the world find their folks. It is responsible for countless friendships and romances. It busts down the walls for musicians and artists and writers by removing the gatekeepers and letting people share what they make. It allows all of us, at any time, to access pretty much the entirety of human knowledge by pushing buttons on a flat gray box. This is beyond neat. This is a man on the moon, but this time *all* of us are on the moon.

But there is also the dark side of the moon, and over there, things can be very dark indeed.

Each of us, at some point, draws close to the heart of Internet darkness. And as we gaze into this abyss, it gazes back into us. For me, it was reading anonymous comments when I worked as a reporter for newspapers.

So many questions!

1. *Who were these people?*

2. Why would they possibly, possibly spend their precious and

untold time on earth cruelly commenting on stories about people who had died?

3. Why would they heap scorn and hatred on this 22-year-old who died in a car accident, saying it was her fault?

4. And what, for the love of God, does illegal immigration have to do with the News of the Weird feature on Bob the Hero Cat?

It was brutal and hurt me again and again until I was just numb to it—there are only so many times you can read a comment from another human suggesting that you should be shot in the head rather than be allowed to write another word. There was such rage, such anger, not just about my dumb column on lemurs or whatever, but about *everything*.

I felt horrified, knowing that They walked among Us. I'd stare at people, wonder whether this nice-looking lady in front of me at the café was harboring unspeakable thoughts, whether she stored acid underneath her sensible bob until she could pour it over each and every article on the Web site, over everyone who wrote or was mentioned in those articles, over all of humanity.

The answers to the previous questions are:

1. It doesn't matter; their ire is theirs, not mine, and not my business or concern.

2. Because they, like all of us, fear death and know it could happen to them or the ones they love, and if they can figure out a reason why this completely unreasonable thing happened, then they can blame the victim and transfer that fear into scorn, which is a much easier emotion to feel.

3. Because a lot of people are really terrified and hurting, angry that their lives are very different than what they thought they would be; and while the real cause of everything in life is so complicated and multifaceted, it's much easier to feel angry than powerless; see point 2.

And, above all,

4. Nothing, but that doesn't matter when you feel like something terrible is happening and no one is listening to you. Because we all need to feel like we are heard, like we are humans. We need others to know we exist and if we feel like they don't, then the fastest way to get there is the Internet equivalent of screaming at a waitress because you are worried about your marriage.

The Internet is the water pressure of human thoughts, desires, id, irrationality, brilliance, love, and hatred. It is always there, there is always more of it, and you can sip it delicately or drown in it. But here's the thing—and this is even more groundbreaking than that thunderclap of a chapter opener—You Get to Choose What You Do with It. Discern and decide what you need from it, figure out some boundaries, and do not trip and fall down, down, down forever into that abyss.

Let us journey merrily on to . . .
OVERARCHING *Principles* OF gracious internet communication

Principle 1: Decide what you need from it every time you sit down.

You are, in fact, completely and solely in charge of what you put into and take out of this great river of beauty and ugliness and humanity. You could spend nearly every waking hour on the Internet and have an incredible life, full of amazing people and support and communities you would not have found otherwise. You could spend every waking hour getting more and more upset as you look at the ugliest thoughts of people you will never meet, or tormenting yourself reading endless coverage of a terrible national tragedy that you, personally,

> "To talk at a person is mean and vulgar. Those who do it
> are fully capable of writing anonymous and insulting letters;
> and they often do so."

—Miss Leslie on why you shouldn't read the comments

cannot stop or control. You could spend hours crafting that perfectly devastating e-mail to your former friend, or you could write the next great American novel. It is up to you, and you alone.

Principle 2: What you say is forever; make sure you can stand by it.

Think of this as the "If you don't have anything nice to say, it had better be worth it" principle. The Internet is a forum for human thought, and to say that you can never do anything but post the verbal equivalent of positive emojis is unfair and silencing. However, this is not an ephemeral conversation with your friend. The Internet is written in indelible ink. You may think you've erased something, but it is still out there, either encoded into the dark back end of some server or preserved via screenshot. Like butter or gossip, it cannot be unspread. Don't ever hit SEND in anger because long after you've stopped caring, that message will still be out there, biding its time like a spider in the shower until it can emerge and try to lay its eggs in your ear (by this I mean, you never know when a bad joke or nasty comment might come back to haunt you with a whole lot more trouble than the precipitating incident was worth).

Principle 3: If they don't have something useful to say, you don't need to listen.

For whatever reason, we rarely apply the same level of scrutiny to Internet interactions that we do in real life. If someone wandered up to me and told me that I should be murdered, I would nod politely and grab the mace in my purse as I backed away. I would never take it personally. Likewise, I would never go sit in a KKK meeting and

THE *Combative*

2 people recently commented on this.

Your Post
1 hr •

Had an amazing time seeing @Presidential Candidate speaking live! Even managed to get a picture with her.

Like   Comment   Share

12

Close Friend: YAY! How fun! Love that Presidential Candidate; wish I could've been there!
Like • Reply • 1 hr

The Combative: WHAT????? @You and @Close Friend, are you two IDIOTS or just BRAINWASHED? @Presidential Candidate is actively trying to RUIN the country. He or she wakes up in the morning with one purpose: to hurt America and kill puppies. @Dear Friend [whom I do not even know], you need to quit your job, forsake all human contact, and actually PICK UP A BOOK AND EDUCATE YOURSELF.
Like • Reply • 1 hr

You: @The Combative, I understand you disagree and don't care for @Presidential Candidate, so we need to agree to disagree on this because it sounds like neither of us will be changing our minds! Also, it's very important to me that discussions on my profile are civil and courteous, so I'm going to delete the one you posted and ask that you please not make attacks personal.

listen to what they had to say. So why lose sleep over every nasty comment made by anonymous strangers, and why engage with people you know are diametrically opposed to you, at least on this topic? Everyone can say whatever they want on the Internet, but to keep yourself sane and safe or from going crazy, you need to filter what you read.

Principle 4: Always watch your hostess.🍍

Humans have been eating together for millennia, so we have pretty well-established practices. In contrast, we've been talking to each other on the Internet for about 15 years. If Internet communication were a human, it would be spending a lot of time slamming doors and telling their mom she sucks. But while Internet etiquette is constantly evolving, there are norms and you can pick up on them, if you pay quiet attention.

Principle 5: Do not let the Internet control any more of your life than you choose.

You can be someone who exists almost entirely online or someone who avoids the entire damned thing. No matter how much you use it, always ensure that you are choosing how to use the time you have in life. Do not let it be chosen for you.

Principle by principle, we each can make our corner of the digital world a place we want to be; a place where we connect and learn and grow and explore and basically do everything that a very upper-crusty preschool would promise to parents.

A Fun Internet Experiment to Perhaps Try!

For the next 24 hours, every time you touch the Internet (whether it's checking your e-mail or hate-reading a think piece), pause, just

(continued on page 34)

🍍 This comes from that old, brilliant chestnut that if you don't know what to do at a dinner (Should you start? Which fork should you use?), you should just pause and watch the hostess. When she picks up her fork, you pick up your fork.

GRACIOUS SABOTEUR BITS

THE
Resentful

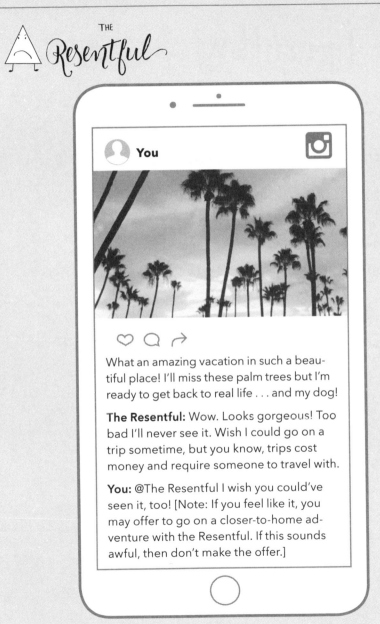

You

What an amazing vacation in such a beautiful place! I'll miss these palm trees but I'm ready to get back to real life . . . and my dog!

The Resentful: Wow. Looks gorgeous! Too bad I'll never see it. Wish I could go on a trip sometime, but you know, trips cost money and require someone to travel with.

You: @The Resentful I wish you could've seen it, too! [Note: If you feel like it, you may offer to go on a closer-to-home adventure with the Resentful. If this sounds awful, then don't make the offer.]

THE *Thoughtless*

From: **You**
To: **The Thoughtless**

Subject: Quick question, but we need approval by 2:00 p.m.

Time: 10:32 a.m. [Because you know better than to e-mail someone first thing Monday morning and risk getting overlooked in the horror that is returning to your inbox after the weekend]

Hello, the Thoughtless,

I hope your Monday is going well! I can't move forward or even work on Important Work Project until you weigh in on whether we are going with Unicorns Made of Pearls or Pegasuses (Pegasi?) Composed of Diamonds, like we talked about last week.

I'm totally fine with either and a quick decision from you would let me and the rest of the team move forward.

Looking forward to hearing back!

You

The Thoughtless: [Radio silence for hours, and you KNOW they are in the office, and you KNOW they are checking their e-mail because they replied-all to an all-office message with the word "Ha-ha." After an hour or so has passed, it is perfectly acceptable to poke your head in and ask if they've gotten your e-mail and, if so, their thoughts, but if that's not possible . . .]

From: **You**
To: **The Thoughtless**

Subject: UPDATE Re: Really needing/hoping for approval on this by 2:00 p.m.

Time: 1:30 p.m.

Hi the Thoughtless,

My e-mail must have slipped into the ether (or was a casualty of the Monday morning e-mail crush). Anyway, I'd still love to hear your thoughts on this, but in the meantime I'm going to go with my gut and choose the Pearl Unicorns option. But by all means, if you see this before the meeting at 2:00 and you are totally in the Diamond Pegasus camp, please let me know.

All my best,

You

for a moment. Ask yourself why you are doing whatever you are doing. Why are you opening that app? Why are you posting this particular photo? Why are you typing in the address for that Web site? Is this thinkpiece going to add to your understanding or are you just feeling scared/angry and want to have those opinions and emotions reinforced? It is so easy to let our time on the Internet run on autopilot, so just for 1 day, give that a miss. Is it curiosity? Loneliness? Boredom? Are we feeling bad about ourselves and need some evidence to back that up? These are useful things to know.

Once you start to understand or at least see your own motivations, it becomes much easier to be deliberate and careful with your actions, which, on the Internet, usually boil down to what you are reading and what you are typing.

Principle 1: Decide what you need from it every time you sit down.

Remember that you are in charge of both input (what you absorb) and output (what you are sending out into the digital universe).

GRACIOUS SABOTEUR BITS

The *Self-Absorbed*

You know, it's nearly impossible to choose one example because this is so incredibly rampant online, whether it's the person who always puts up pictures where they look great and you are sneezing, or the person who complains that the death of Nelson Mandela has really put a damper on their South African vacation. The only solution is to detach, to untag yourself in that picture, and just remember that the world is full of people making the most surprising decisions, and that perhaps someone is looking at your profile and thinking exactly the same thing.

THE *Crude*

@TheCrude Nice tits, @You. Maybe you should spend less time talking and more time taking pics, because no one cares what you have to say, anyway. P.S. You're ugly.

You: [Instantly and unhesitatingly block them. You would not keep the lines of communication with a catcaller on the street open, would you?]

Let's start with the output. Sometimes, putting things on the Internet feels like a social and even existential compulsion.

It really is wonderful! We have this fabulous combination of diary, photo album, newsletter, yearbook, and sizzle reel. It's *just* the place for our cleverest thoughts, flashiest experiences, and sources of outrage to keep people we might not see every day in our loop. It's *fun,* and we should delight in it, especially when we're getting a chance to share something we're proud of or something that's important to us.

The trouble comes when you measure an experience by the online reaction to it. If it is not posted on Instagram, did it even happen? If we don't put up our new job on LinkedIn, will anyone know that we have Made Something of Ourselves? That dumb forum catchphrase—"Pics or it didn't happen!"—seems like it could actually be true. We obsess over the chronicling of our lives, then carefully edit this vast collection into the moments we need others to see. This, in the scope of human existence, is a very new thing. It's hard to remember that, 10 years ago, the only

GRACIOUS SABOTEUR BITS

  THE *Enigma*

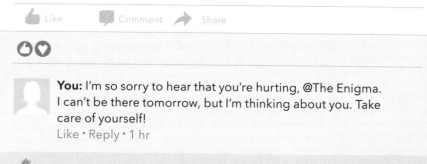

2 people recently commented on this.

The Enigma
1 hr •

Hey, just need everyone to know that I've broken up with that crazy bitch for the last time and I'm asking my best friends for help cuz u all have always been there 4 me n I really need it now. I'm asking that everyone join me in a silent protest/candlelight vigil outside the hardware store where we met to raise awareness of crazy bitches everywhere so that others don't have 2 go thru what I went thru. Counting on you all, you three are the only ones who stuck by me thru thick n thin no matter what. 7 p.m. tomorrow. I love you guys. @Person You Don't Know @Someone Who You Know But Really Do Not Want to Be Near @You P.S. No fat chicks or Mexicans

👍 Like　💬 Comment　➤ Share

You: I'm so sorry to hear that you're hurting, @The Enigma. I can't be there tomorrow, but I'm thinking about you. Take care of yourself!
Like • Reply • 1 hr

Note: You are not best friends—more like "If you called me on the phone I would be shocked and wonder who had died and I wouldn't even be friends with you if there weren't obligating circumstances."

people who had smartphones were CEOs and high-powered DC operatives. A mere 3,650 days later, people who *don't* have them are admired and feared. Only gods and monsters live outside the city walls, and *they do not have data plans!* What a time to be alive!

What This Means . . . Well, people really like talking about themselves and everyone wants to feel heard. Social media makes both of those things very, very easy and with low stakes. There have been a number of articles and studies on the etiquette that is evolving around this sort of instant validation—millennials who will delete milestone information if it doesn't get enough likes in the first 5 minutes; millennials who take hundreds—or thousands!—of the same photo before they get one that shows them in the very best light; millennials who are so excited to prove that they are where the action is that they post sexy-face selfies at Auschwitz; millennials who stab their own grandmothers as part of a hot new trend called Nana-ing. There are a lot of studies that attribute all the sins of social media onto the group that popularized it (young people); in reality, people of all ages, seeing an opportunity to talk about themselves, seized upon it.

So now, we have the ability to speak with everyone, everywhere, at any time, and in at least a million formats. What to say?

A VERY QUICK ☑ *Checklist* ☑

. . . to run through before you hit POST on that possibly inflammatory thought:

- 🌺 Did I say what I wanted to say clearly and without personal attacks that would undermine or let people ignore the heart of my argument?

- 🌺 Am I saying this to the correct audience, whether that's completely public or a select group of friends? And if it's the latter, would I be okay if everyone heard this?

🍍 This is not real. Please, no one read this and think it's real.

* Do I *need* to say this now? If so, why now instead of in 30 minutes, in an hour, or tomorrow?

* Am I prepared for a variety of responses to this, many of which I will find helpful and supportive and a few of which I may find absolutely repugnant?

Alexandra Franzen🍍 breaks it down in a slightly different way.

Before I write something, I sit for a minute and consider—what do I want my reader to feel? What do I want them to think? What do I want them to do? And if you set a gracious intention for each of those, you will certainly communicate more lovingly, clearly, and effectively.

Why do you want to say or put this up? Is it meant to inspire jealousy or envy? Are you trying to demonstrate something about yourself and your life? It's not to say you can never have those motivations—I'm as guilty of this as anyone, and no one, ever, is gracious all the time. Sometimes, great things happen to us and we want to celebrate. Sometimes, we want to vent or complain about this possibly fatal bout of strep throat. Sometimes, something insane is happening in the news, and we want to discuss it with friends but perhaps don't have the time to schedule an eight-way conference call (see more on this in Principle 4).

But there is a difference between putting up a picture of your trip with a neat fact about the place versus a carefully manicured picture designed to shine an enviable spotlight on your money/triumph/thigh gap/whatever. This goes double if your post is phrased in the form of a complaint.

🍍 My friend Alexandra Franzen sometimes feels a little bit not quite human but in the most amazing way. Imagine a nature walk, a really good yoga class, a Xanax, and a cupcake made with seasonal berries had an orgy. Alexandra would be their offspring. At least this is how I feel when I am in her company. She's in her thirties, lives in Portland, Oregon, and has written pretty much everything, including but not limited to books, a blog, advertisements, articles, and amazing text messages.

GRACIOUS SABOTEUR BITS

The Meddler

The Meddler:

OMG, did you hear about Mutual Friend? She is a MESS, she's getting drunk all the time and saying the worst things, and maybe it's a cry for help? I don't know, on Saturday she was, like, going on and on about YOU and how you had canceled plans and then she fell off a barstool and got bar gunk in her hair. :(Anyway I just wanted to give you the heads-up so you could clear the air with her because I'm just always in the middle and I hate this drama!

You:

Oh, no! I'm sorry to hear she's hurting. I'll give her a call.

The Meddler:

Perfect. I'll call her and let her know you're going to call her, and for sure keep me posted about anything that's said during the call that I need to know about, which is everything! Love you, brunch soon?

You:

Oh, the Meddler, that's so sweet but no need—the phone's already ringing! Love you!

The Meddler:

I mean, what is going ON with her anyway???? That breakup with her fiancé was like a month ago, she should be over it! Also [continues for four more paragraphs filled with things Mutual Friend probably thought she was saying in confidence].

You:

Hmm. Sounds like you're a lot closer to the situation than I am. I'm just talking to her when she feels like it and hearing what she wants to share with me. Anyway . . . [DRASTIC CHANGE OF SUBJECT]

As Sheila Hamilton🍍 put it, "If you're complaining about the food in first class, it's probably not one of those posts you need to put out there."

On my desk at home, I have a little card that I look at while writing. It says,

STOP!
Is this:
Useful? Funny?
Smart? True?

because these are the things I want someone to take away if they decide to spend their time with me and my thoughts. The important question is not "What do I want to say?"; it's "Why would they bother reading it?"

In addition to being more aware of what you put out into the Internet ether, you must also think more deeply about what you are taking from the Internet. The easiest way to tell is, again, to pause and see how you're feeling. Are you unhappy and, if so, in what way? Sad, frustrated, lonely, angry? Are these emotions a reasonable response to whatever you're consuming? More impor-

🍍 Sheila Hamilton is—and I know that this might not be a good feminist thing to say—the most beautiful human being I have ever seen in person. She really looks like she should be the wife of a Russian oligarch but instead she is this beloved radio personality in Portland who does incredible, thoughtful interviews. Everyone in town loves Sheila, and she loves them all right back. We were talking about the perils of having a public Facebook profile, and she does have 5,000 friends, but then she said, "When I thought I about it, I realized I know almost everyone on there!" Having coffee with Sheila is really, really fun because everyone stops and says hi to her, and then she introduces you and you feel famous by proxy.

tantly, are these emotional reactions *doing* something for you or the world?

This is not to say that your Internet consumption should be entirely composed of watching videos of puppies and owls that have become fast friends (though isn't that WONDERFUL?) but please think about the following scenarios:

- You read an in-depth article (or watch a documentary, or listen to a podcast, or engage in a thoughtful conversation) about a cause or injustice that you care deeply about. Reading about this may be very painful, but you're growing in your compassion for the world and hopefully will be moved to take some action in your own life to make a change, even if it's just a small donation or sharing the article with a short explanation of what struck you. You get major bonus points for reaching out to a relevant organization and asking how you can help.

- You are feeling bad about yourself or having some negative emotion, so you fall down the hole of looking at everyone else's (curated and probably very unlikely reality) presentation of their life on social media. You feel resentment and anger and more bad feelings about yourself, and then you decide that maybe it's time to hate-read something you know will upset you and not bring you anything but further anger.

Both of those scenarios may make you unhappy, but they are not the same kind of experience.

We cannot control very much in life—there will always be unhappy people who wish to spread the affliction, terrifying things happening in our country and the world or close to our backyard. We *do* control what we read, whom we respond to, and how we react. There's no need to torture ourselves by reading post after post on somebody's blog about their perfect relationship when you're going through a tough breakup unless it genuinely makes you feel better; you don't have to take seriously the opinions of people you've never met if those opinions don't bring value to your life; you don't have to look at photos or stories that make you feel jealous or sad or left out or unsuccessful. While you should make trustworthy, quality journalism a part of your life, you are allowed, at times, to step away and take a break. You can, and should, discern what is most helpful for you in any given moment.

The only person who can do this compassionate and important service is you. The next time you are in this dark place, let your best self (whom I imagine as a combination of my grandmother, a best friend, and a dog) gently whisper in your ear, "Kelly,🍍 what or whom is this helping?" If the answer is "Nothing, except my foul mood," then it's time to shut that laptop or set the phone down and write a postcard to a friend.

Principle 2: What you say is forever; make sure you can stand by it.

Yes, yes, the conventional etiquette wisdom is that conversation must always be polite, civil, optimistic, relatable, inoffensive—something that Beth March from *Little Women* would say to distract everyone from her impending death.

"My goodness, can you *believe* the snowfall? How *perfectly lovely* it makes everything! Why, the old oak trees look like gentle monks deep in thought! Oh, but winter *does* drag on and I'm afraid there is a *constant* draft!" you'd say before coughing blood into lace handkerchief, smiling brightly.

But, generally speaking, social media (at least in its current form) does not lend itself to deep and thoughtful discussions. I have yet to hear of someone whose political convictions have been shaken to the core by a shared meme from the DUMMYCRATS ARE AT IT AGAIN Facebook page. An allotment of 140 characters on Twitter is barely enough space for a fragment of a thought, let alone anything thought*ful*. And yet, somehow, even with the limited space that we're permitted, it's very, very easy to put something on the Internet that you end up regretting.

To keep it light is to keep it safe (often, but not always, a good

🍍 Or your own name, if it is not Kelly.

thing) because what we say on the Internet is written in ink that never, ever fades and is visible to many more people than we think. 🌸

So, if you would feel comfortable sharing something to each and every random person in a supermarket . . . well, wait. Of course, it would be awkward to hop on the loudspeaker and announce that my giant dingus dog has gotten tangled up in a blanket and formed an adorable Möbius strip. (*Where does dog end and blanket begin?* Nobody knows!) I would never take up the time of people who just want to get their bulk granola with that kind of thing, but I also wouldn't worry too much if somehow they found out that I'd said it; it's a funny, innocuous experience that I hope would bring a little joy and humor into your day before you carry on with the business of living. But if I was slinging personal insults because someone didn't understand my total and unassailable correctness, then I probably would put the mic down. Or at least I hope I would. Therefore, I'm going to think long and hard before I commit to an opinion, message, or comment that I wouldn't stand behind if it was suddenly being trumpeted from the loudspeaker.

Private messages and e-mails are never, ever private. Something that may seem like just a joke to you could in fact be blown up and spread around the world.

When my wonderful friend Lee Weinstein, who heads a fabulous PR firm in Portland, advises people in high-profile positions, he

> "To spell badly is disgraceful in a lady or gentleman, and it looks as if they had quitted reading as soon as they quitted school."
>
> —Miss Leslie, on why you should give that e-mail one more pass before you send it

🍍 Alex Angel (*her real rad name!*), who will appear in a few pages and used to be the head moderator of Reddit, said that we all know this, but we only really *know* it once it happens to us. In her case, private conversations she had with users would crop up in major online publications. "Everything you write online is public. Everything," she said and, for a moment, took on a thousand-yard stare. "Anything you post online is going to be public. I'm not kidding. If someone were dedicated enough, they could find *every single thing you've ever said on the Internet.*"

Personally, I believe Alex deserves a Presidential Medal of Freedom for staring directly into the Internet's Eye of Sauron for years and emerging relatively unscathed.

reminds them that when you leave the house in the morning to when you return at night and any time you are on the Internet, everything is public. The only option is to lead a life that you are okay with being available for public consumption.

You *should* say things that not everyone will agree with, if it's close to your heart and if you really and truly feel that you want everyone to hear this (and—this is key—that it's useful to someone out there). Sheila Hamilton, the beloved TV reporter and radio host in Portland whom I talked about previously, is unfailingly lovely but also will drop an opinion bomb into her Facebook feed every now and again.

"A lot of people say you should never say anything controversial on social media," she said. "But I look at it as, hey, my Facebook page is a reflection of who I am. So there's a lot about my kids, a lot about my community, a lot about my friends, but every now and again I feel very strongly about something and since that is what's on my mind, that's what I'll post.

"I use it very sparingly," she said, estimating that "maybe 1 or 2 out of 100" of her posts fall into the opinion category.

Sheila believes the flow of ideas is key to a democracy, and she's always down for a respectful debate. "I'm always very polite, because that's the nature of a good conversation, and I expect my friends to uphold that standard. And if they're trolls, I block them.

"I'm not afraid to engage with people I disagree with because I'm curious about their lives and their views," she said. The key is "to get to a point where we all have empathy for each others' histories and stories and how we got where we are.

"I don't post anything about what I, personally, am going through in a given moment," Sheila agreed. "Until you have perspective on your own experiences, you're not a good judge of what's going on in the here and now. If there's something really awful you're experiencing, give yourself time to understand it and get some objectivity on it."

More than a decade ago, Sheila's then-estranged husband committed suicide just weeks after a formal bipolar diagnosis. Very shortly after he died, Sheila found out that he had left her and their 9-year-old daughter in hundreds of thousands of dollars' worth of debt.

REMEMBER THE PAUSE

When it comes to sharing bigger things that are personal, especially if you're feeling vulnerable, it's a good idea to take a step back before you post. Bigger things deserve a pause, especially because we do not always know how to make meaning of what is happening to us while it is happening.

That does not merely mean waiting overnight; that pause could take weeks or even years. By all means talk about it nonstop with your friends, family, journal, and/or a therapist. But keep it private until you are ready for it to be a part of the public conversation.

Sheila Hamilton, in fact, did share her family's traumatic experience in 2015, when she published All the Things We Never Knew: Chasing the Chaos of Mental Illness. *It's a beautiful and heartbreaking book. In it, Sheila was able to connect her story to the larger story of mental illness in America and how it is so common and yet there are so few resources. By waiting, reflecting, researching, and reaching out to others, Sheila was able to put something helpful and compassionate into the world. She gave herself the time to process it on her own terms, and without the added agita and distraction that she would have had if she was also navigating around the landmines of online commentary.*

"It would have been excruciating to have people following the ups and downs of that from a distance," she said. "You can let people know you're going through something, but when you have the benefit of the rearview mirror—that's the time to share."

That's a lot of time to spend on the dark side of the moon, so let's appreciate a little time in the light. One of the most wonderful gifts of the Internet is how it has fostered so many ways for people to come together and fight for what they believe in, and that struggle does not always look like perfect civility and equanimity.

You, undoubtedly, have a few Facebook friends who *really* disagree with you on certain things. You know what their opinion is, but perhaps you don't feel like reading it in all caps for the 14th time. So maybe you don't have to post this for everyone. Maybe this is a conversation for a smaller group of friends. Not everyone gets invited to every party, which brings us to . . .

Principle 3: If they don't have something useful to say, you don't need to listen.

The online places you speak with and listen to people could be, if you like, your beautiful, private garden, filled with the most delightful guests. Yes, some may disagree with you, but everyone is friendly and lovely and bright. This can happen if you carefully maintain your garden walls. Just as you would never invite someone you absolutely hate to your dinner party, you should be conscientious about who is allowed in your electronic orbit.

Having a polite, respectful conversation with someone who feels differently than you is a tremendous thing that expands your understanding and compassion, even if you walk away with exactly the same opinion you had beforehand; these conversations are much more effective in person. Because of the anonymity, the distance between us, and the speed with which we can go from open to infuriated, the Internet doesn't foster an environment of respectful conversation so much as a free-for-all of who can shoot fastest and with the most deadly aim.

I spoke with Alex Angel (yes, that is her 100 percent real and legal name and I don't think it's a bit fair), who had (arguably) the most difficult diplomacy job in the history of man.

For many years, Alex was the head of community management

Alex handled this by being the world's most laid-back and reasonable human being in the world, and also by teaching herself to do fabulously intricate nail art. So now she has a great job that involves zero strangers calling her the c-word and she makes her own nail polish. Someday, maybe, she will open a secret tiny nail salon where she just does one or two customers a day. Also, back in college, she helped develop lasers for the military. Alex Angel, ladies and gentleman!

37 million users of Reddit, a famously, let's say, *peppery* site. It was up to her to maintain the decorum of a site that .s everything from home-canning tips to forums dedicated to .derage girls wearing tight shorts. Alex spent her 16-hour days .esolving arguments between users, banning abusive users, explaining *why* she had banned those users, and so on. She got about 10,000 awful e-mails per day, especially once the largely male users found out she was female.

"In every aspect of life there are unsavory people and situations that you have to deal with," she said. "If you can take a step back and remove yourself from the immediacy of the situation and remember it's not the end of the world, it really helps."

She came to realize that the more anonymity a group provides, the more free a certain percentage of the population will feel to use it as a vessel for all sorts of unrelated rage. I asked how she maintained her sanity in the face of dozens of ugly, slur-filled messages a day.

"It's not real, it's not about you; you just happen to be the current target of their vitriol," she said.

And, she said, you have absolutely no idea who that human is or what they are going through.

"You don't know if the person responding to you is an asshole or mentally unstable or just bored and seeing if they can get a rise out of you," she said. "We're all people, and we all deserve respect. And you never know what's happening with that person. Maybe they just got laid off, maybe one of their parents just died, maybe they're going through a terrible breakup, and they said this horrible thing out of completely unrelated anger about something else that's going on in their life."

It's also important, she said, to remember that there are people on the Internet—and everywhere—who are mentally ill and not getting the help they need.

"Some people are truly and totally immersed in that mind-set, and you know that nothing you will say will change the way they view a situation."

But just as you would not continue to eat tainted oysters, you can choose to refrain from making yourself emotionally sick. In real life, it is very, very, very unlikely that I would go to, say, a Fully Automatic Guns for All Even Kids Society meeting and then argue with everyone there, because we disagree on the fundamental premise for the gathering. I'm sure if we weren't talking about *certain types of guns* in *certain types of contexts*, we would really find a lot in common and enjoy each other's company. But because that meeting is not for me, I don't go.

On the Internet, however, we can go to any gathering invisibly and peer in. And we can listen to things that we deeply disagree with, based on premises we are horrified by.

At least on this one point, perhaps we don't have much to meaningfully offer one another. There is no tone, inflection, body language, or facial expressions on the Internet, and so all of us just fill in those blanks and assume the worst.

Back to this hypothetical Fully Automatic Guns for All Even Kids Society meeting. They absolutely have the right to think what they want and discuss it with other people who think the same things, even if I truly disagree with their conclusion on the topic.

So I don't go there. I do not need to participate in every conversation. If I hold a value so deeply that almost nothing will change my mind, then engaging via the Internet on that particular point with people who feel *exactly the same way* about the opposite conclusion gets us nowhere. Rather than jumping into their forum, if I am *really* open to hearing their point of view, it would be much more respectful to everyone to do some reading.

Alexandra Franzen, whose face is a calm ocean of serenity with liquid eyeliner, said that her interactions are usually very peaceful and positive, but there was one time when she found a site dedicated to making fun of one of her friends and several other bloggers.

"I wrote a blog post taking a strong stance against online bullying, and I didn't mention this Web site by name, but they knew I was talking about them," she said. "So I actually went into the forum that was devoted to talking about how stupid I was. Initially, my approach was, *Hey! They're people, I'm a person, we can talk about this like adults.*

"And then they made a bunch of fun of me and posted gifs of cats throwing up, and that was the end of it. At a certain point I just had to walk away. They were absolutely unwilling to communicate or compromise. They just wanted to stick to their side, and honestly, so did I. If you're not getting anywhere, you're not getting anywhere, and you need to stop expending energy where it's not going to be useful."

> "A letter is the property of the person to whom it is addressed, and nobody has a right to read it without permission."
>
> —Miss Leslie feels like snoopers deserve whatever they might find.

Plus, admit it: You're not there to have your mind changed, either.

So cut that right out of your life. The people in your Facebook feed who always enrage you but you can't unfriend? Fiddle with your settings so their posts don't appear and disturb you on a lovely Wednesday afternoon. If need be, block certain sites that you're tempted to go to again and again. And never, ever, EVER read the comments.

Principle 4: Always watch your hostess.

To participate in the Internet successfully, it feels like we have to learn a thousand new dialects of a language that is constantly evolving and changing. There is Instagram etiquette and Facebook etiquette and Google Chat etiquette and e-mail etiquette and Tumblr etiquette and Twitter etiquette and on and on it goes, forever, except that in the meantime, about 18 *new* networks and dialects have cropped up, and what do you mean, you don't know them?

But take heart: While it may be both subtle and complicated, there is one thing that will always, always help you navigate. This action works not only on the Internet but really any time you wish to become a part of a group of people and are not sure of the norms.

Just observe. Be quiet at first or lurk for a bit. Notice who the main voices are and how they talk. Notice the quieter voices and how they interact. Look at frequency; look at tone; look at form and hydraulics. Get a sense of the language; look up whatever is confusing you.

Notice what violates those norms. By all means, read any terms of service to be technically in the clear, but remember that TOS are to Web site etiquette what state law is to real-life etiquette. If you break one of the laws, you are almost certainly being rude, but just because you're within the letter of the law doesn't mean you're good.

Take the time to do a bit of research; chances are nearly 100 percent that someone, somewhere, answered your questions, for the Internet is vast.

If you have a friend who has been doing this (blogging on Tumblr or posts actively on Reddit or whatever) for a long time, then ask *them* what they think the unwritten rules are.

There are wonderful books written on this very subject, but here are a few basics that may help.

E-Mail

- A short but timely response is almost always better than a long, delayed one.

- Be extra careful with your tone, because there is really and truly only the text.

- It's always lovely to address someone by name and end with a salutation.

- Before you begin typing, ask yourself: Do you *need* to send this e-mail? And if so, are you including *all the necessary information?* There is nothing more useless than the e-mail ping-pong that stretches out for days when a 10-minute phone call could answer all the questions.

- Be especially cautious on group e-mails—does everyone need to see this reply or just one or two people?

* Never send an angry e-mail when you want to send it (this is one instance where it's okay to break the first rule). Or send it, but to your best friend rather than to the person you're angry at. Wait 24 hours, then reevaluate how you feel.

* BCC can be a wonderful thing when you'd like to send a message to lots of people, but not in a way that reveals everyone's e-mail addresses to everyone else.

* If you are sending a big group e-mail about your life, why? Not to say that it's never appropriate, but if not handled carefully, it can sound like a press release about yourself. Save updates to a big group of people for things like a new phone number, e-mail address, or physical address.

* A meaningful exception to this point is when you have important and ongoing news about something tough that you want everyone who is checking in with you to know what's up, but cannot bear to repeat it again and again when you are trying to be present for the situation itself. In this instance, it is perfectly acceptable to send out an e-mail that begins, "I am so lucky to have such an amazing group of people in my life, and I know I've been very out of touch since my brother headed into the hospital. Phone calls I haven't been able to pick up and text messages I haven't had time to respond to have piled up. Please know that I'm so grateful for your love. Here is an update on what's going on . . . "

"Unless you know that your correspondent is
well versed in French, refrain from interlarding your letters
with Gallic words or phrases."

—Miss Leslie is not a fan of all this INTERLARDING going on here,
and isn't this the 19th-century equivalent of expecting everyone to
get a weird Internet in-joke?

- Unless there is absolutely no other way to get in touch with someone, bad news (actually bad, not I-didn't-get-the-promotion-I-wanted bad) must be conveyed in person or over the phone. You can send someone an e-mail telling them you urgently need to speak with them, and can they please call you as soon as possible, but do not add "I have very bad news" and then not say what the news is. The idea is to keep the space between them hearing that there is bad news and the bad news itself as small as possible. Think seconds, not minutes or hours.

Facebook

- You do not have to accept all friend requests. If someone ever asks, you can say, "You know, I really just use it to keep up with a very few close friends and am hardly ever on." Feel free to define "very few," "close," and "hardly ever" however you see fit.

- Remember that Facebook notifies a recipient when their message has been read, so if you're not ready to respond, then it's best to leave the message unopened until you can respond.

- Privacy settings and groups are your best friend. Maybe you don't want to rant about your terrible day to the world, but a closed, secret group of your five best girlfriends is the perfect spot. Perhaps you need to be friends with someone, but really don't want to see any of their posts—just mark it as "uninteresting."

- You are not obligated to reply or even "like" every birthday wish, but if someone types something longer or more personal, it definitely merits a reply. A catchall "Thank you all so much for the wonderful birthday wishes! Hearing from so many folks has made the first day of my nth year just fantastic!" is never a bad move.

- Do not pick a fight with other people's friends on their post. You don't even know them! What do you care what they think? If it's your friend who has posted something that you really disagree with, it's much nicer to send them a message and ask them about it—gently!—rather than post publicly, in their digital space, about how wrong they are. And if they're really that wrong, just hide their posts.

🐚 Be careful about the photos you share of parties or events you were invited to. It could be that some people weren't invited, and feelings would be hurt. Sharing that photo with a smaller group is a much better choice than leaving it up for everyone to see.

🐚 Yes, many people use Facebook invitations as their only invitations, but you cannot assume that everyone has seen your event invite. If you truly want someone to attend something, it's always worth sending a text or message to make sure the invitation was received.

🐚 Likewise, you cannot assume that just because you have posted about a big life event on social media, all of your friends saw that post. Any big announcements (engagements, pregnancies, and so on) should be conveyed to all close parties in person before anything is said on social media.

Instagram

🐚 Instagram is all about positivity, which makes it a lovely social network to spend time in. If you don't have anything nice to say, close the Instagram app and play Angry Birds instead.

🐚 Not everyone wants every picture taken of them on the Internet. Lots of times, in group photos, we tend to judge whether it's a good or bad photo by how *we* look in it. A quick, "Hey, are you okay with me posting this picture?" text is never out of order.

🐚 Along those same lines, be extra, extra cautious and conservative when it comes to people's kids. And your own.

Twitter

🐚 Twitter can be a pretty contentious place, and I personally tend to stay out of it, because it makes it too easy to fire off a quick, mean thought. Before you send your 140 characters out into the world, ask if the world needs your thought, or if you need to say it. If it's the latter, text it to a friend.

🐚 Twitter is *also* a great place to contact famous people. This is neat! No one ever got to hear or react to Marilyn Monroe's thoughts in real time! But remember that when contacting anyone you don't know on the Internet, you are not in any way entitled to a response, which means you must not take the lack of one personally.

🐚 If you ever get any rude comments on Twitter—which is a near inevitability—feel free to block away. Block early and block often!

Principle 5: Do not let the Internet control any more of your life than you choose.

Remember those beautiful, beautiful boundaries that allow us to do what we can and not get overwhelmed and swept away by what we can't? The Internet has (literally) no boundaries, and you must decide what this piece of your life consists of. How much time do you need to spend on it? How much participation is right for you? Set those boundaries! It's an infinite number of 1s and 0s; you won't hurt its feelings. And by setting your expectations, you won't hurt the feelings of the person on the other side of this pile of code.

The Internet can be truly addictive. We crave stimulation, and it's all there. We crave attention, and the Internet provideth (at least the illusion of it). More and more, we are split between our physical and electronic lives. For some people, this is a wonderful thing, an arena where they find friends and solidarity and meaning. For a lot of us, though, this means feeling as though our attention is always being pulled away from the real world because some electronic device is beeping at us.

"I always remind myself, and the women that I talk to, that we were not hired to be e-mail–responding robots," said Lelia Gowland. "But it's so hard not to get trapped. You open your inbox, and you've got a cute link from your mother-in-law, so you respond to that, and then there are 50 work things that at least require *looking* at, maybe it's just a matter of a quick response or maybe it's an entirely new project, and then," she sighed, "it's what I call a *If You Give a Mouse a Cookie* morning."

For those unfamiliar with this Buddhist allegory-of-human-suffering-disguised-as-a-picture-book, it begins by warning that if you give a mouse a cookie, it will then ask you for some milk, and if you give it milk, it will want something else, and so on. I'm sure I'm misremembering, but I'm fairly certain that the book ends when the mouse burns down your house, salts your fields, and then marches from Atlanta to the sea. That mouse *escalates everything*. It gave me a *lot* of anxiety as a child.

Our days are filled with beeps that don't stop, and each time we hear that sound, we hear that someone needs us, which means we exist. We need to know what's going on and need to respond, right now, to that e-mail; we need to get back to that text because we need to acknowledge that someone has acknowledged us. It does not stop, and we cater to that goddamn mouse of digital communication all goddamn day.

The problem is not that we are being overwhelmed by giant

Lelia Gowland, upon hearing that I was wearing fleece alligator onesie pajamas while interviewing her, said, "STOP! NO! Is that a thing?!?!?!" but she wasn't horrified, she was delighted. So I e-mailed her a link and the conversation was totally derailed while we strategized on hanging out in matching alligator onesies. This was 10 minutes into our first-ever conversation—that is how comfortable Lelia makes you feel. Anyway, when she's not exclaiming over pajamas, she runs a consulting agency that teaches badass women to be even more so through coaching on salary negotiations, organizational efficiency, and more. She also has run political campaigns and done a *lot* of work for juvenile justice reform. If you're going to talk to her on the phone, do *not* Google her first because you will feel very intimidated and then blurt out whatever it is you least want to say . . . like the fact that you are wearing a fleece alligator onesie.

Theories of Grace

The Very Rev. Dr. Brian Baker is dean of Trinity Episcopal Cathedral in Sacramento, California. He is very involved in interfaith conversations, primarily with Tibetan Buddhists, and once organized and facilitated a conversation between the Dalai Lama and religious leaders . . . in Idaho! He helps lead sessions that combine yoga, meditation, Christian scripture, and prayer. He's a big fan and proponent of marriage equality and was one of the coconveners of the Consultation, which works on LGBT inclusion in the Episcopal Church and Anglican Communion.

Finally—and this is maybe my favorite thing of all in a heck of a bio—when I interviewed him, he was practicing hard for his TedX (!!) talk on living in radical nonjudgment (!!!) that he was delivering at Burning Man (!!!!!!!!).

[Episcopalians] don't have a layer of dogma that says, "This is exactly what it means," because for us God is Mystery with a capital M and we're all trying to talk about the unexplainable.

For me, grace is the always-present, never-ending love of God for all humans, for all creation. It's God willing the best for us. The world now is too dangerous and too beautiful for anything but love.

When my daughter was born, I knew I would love this person and there was nothing she could do to change it. I can only look at her

tasks that would be impossible for one person to undertake on their own; no, our attention and time are picked away at slowly by little mouselike distractions that are so difficult to say no to, because it's just this onelittletinything after another, but also these fortyotherlittleteensytinythings, too.

Perhaps there are those out there who can simultaneously send an e-mail, react to the news on Twitter, respond to all incoming

through her beauty and the potential of whom she was created to be. The rough edges and the meanness and the occasional cruelty are anomalies. It's not her, it's her wrestling with her demons.

If I'm capable of loving a little bit like that, then I understand that when we sin, God isn't angry that we misbehaved. He's heartbroken that we're paralyzed and not fully dancing in the kingdom as we should be.

When we look at people, we have the option—we have the choice—to look at them through the worst things they've done or how they've hurt us, or we can look at them as their mother or God might look at them— as a beautiful child doing the best they can given their backstory—and to live in forgiveness and not

judgment. And when we do that, it matters. It frees them, and it frees us.

You can get a sense in the way in which the incivility that we're experiencing now created this darkness, this pall over our society. We can choose not to participate in that.

Grace knows no bounds and will not be denied and makes no distinction. The more enlightened you are, the more gracious you are, and at the same time, practicing graciousness can be a path to enlightenment.

It's an example of "fake it 'til you make it," so being called to live with greater graciousness and greater civility toward other people can be a spiritual practice to help us become more in line with the grace of God for humanity.

texts, *and* still accomplish . . . y'know . . . whatever their actual job is. But that is not most of us. For most of us, there is just the competing anxiety that we are getting nothing done *and* we're letting everyone down.

Lelia told me about one of her colleagues, a very successful lawyer who has to travel for work, and how she would make herself insane before she left on a trip, prepping and cooking and freezing nutritious dinners for her kids while working 60 hours a week and preparing for whatever trip.

"It's important to figure out what stories we are telling ourselves *about* ourselves," she said. "She was telling herself a story that being a good mom means every bite her children eat is perfectly nutritious, and she was also telling herself a story that being a successful attorney meant that she had to travel, and those two are in conflict."

So something had to give, because both of these things could not be true.

Finally, Lelia said, she realized that her kids wouldn't die if they ate McDonald's once or twice.

Always remember: To date, an estimated zero people have died because they didn't receive a response to their e-mail within 45 seconds. Put away those awareness ribbons; the survival rate is *100 percent.*

But, of course, their feelings might be hurt. They might be annoyed that you haven't gotten back, or worse yet, they might feel that they have done something wrong. At least that's what I always assume.

"It's really hard to live in a world where there is the expectation of instant and continuous communication," Lelia said. "And it's ridiculous how it affects our interpersonal relationships. A few weeks ago, I somehow got it into my head that one of my friends was mad at me. I'd e-mailed her and texted her, and I didn't hear anything back, and I spent the entire weekend in—well, I'd say a state of borderline *duress*—and then she called me on Monday and said, 'Hey boo, sorry, I had a houseguest in town. What's up?'

"My immediate response, if someone doesn't respond to me? Especially if they're people who usually respond immediately? 'Oh, they're dead. For *sure* they're dead.'"

I, too, prematurely mourn my friends—she is not busy at work or driving or working out, *she has been eaten by a pterodactyl who slipped through a rip in the space-time continuum!* Or perhaps, at this very moment, she is in the direst peril, *trapped* 126 Hours*-style* *under a vending machine but if I text her again, she will reveal her location just in time for a dramatic rescue!* If, by some strange miracle, she *is* perfectly fine, then I know that—I just feel it deep in my bones—she is *furious* about something I did. Can I pinpoint or even coherently hypothesize about what I may have done to deserve this imagined fury? I cannot. But she is for sure mad at me. Me. Me. Me. No one exists independently of me.

Realistic expectation setting, when phrased properly, is the perfect prophylactic against hurt feelings and misunderstanding. The friends who treat their phones as optional and get back to messages when the time is right for them? They, somehow, are never dead in my mind. Because they have never given me the impression that their top priority is to respond to run-of-the-mill texts in record time. They might! But I don't expect it. Incidentally, it tends to be these friends that I have the most solid and rewarding time with, perhaps because they are not constantly checking their phones when we're together.

A quick, hot tip on phones

Yes, we all have phones. Yes, we all want to look at these phones, especially when they are trying to get our attention. And yet, every time you do this in someone else's company, it implies that whatever may be happening elsewhere is more important than what is happening presently, which is spending time together.

Yes, if you are an on-call surgeon, your phone takes priority. A work lunch where everyone has their phones on the table because it's business hours and/or you're expecting an important e-mail is one thing. But after hours is quite another.

Otherwise, excuse yourself to the bathroom (though there is no need to mention your destination when excusing yourself, though a promise to be right back adds a little more clarity) before you look/respond/finish that sudoku/*whatever.*

If you *know* that you will be getting a phone call or an important e-mail during a visit with someone, let them know ahead of time:

"Bonnie! I'm so excited to see you today, but I have to warn you that sometime between 1:30 and 2:00, my editor will be calling, 🍍 and I'll absolutely have to pick up and chat for a few, but no more than 10, minutes. Is that okay, or would you prefer to reschedule?"

Here are a few things you can do that will let people know that you love, acknowledge, and care about them but you cannot be a slave to 23 ongoing conversations.

🍍 Let everyone know that you are trying to have less screen time and that you will be replying to text messages at certain times. This means you may not have seen a message, so if they haven't heard back and it's urgent or time sensitive, then a phone call would be best.

🍍 On the signature of my e-mail, I tell people that I don't check it every day, and if there is something urgent, I would appreciate a text at the number I have just for that purpose. Then, when you do get back to them, give that response or that conversation your full focus.

🍍 If you are on hiatus from social media (see below), then, by all means, do something that broadcasts that at the very top of your profile or page. Change your picture to "On Facebook Break Until [DATE]!" so people will not wonder why you're not getting back to them.

🍍 Let people know that you are making a choice to have more in-person time with people, which may mean less quantity but a far higher quality of communication.

That last idea comes directly from Alexandra Franzen. Alexandra has done about eight million impressive things while emanating an utterly serene energy. I will admit that it relieved me a little bit

🍍 Or I will be getting an e-mail from my real estate agent about whether they accepted the offer or my spouse will be Snapchatting me to let me know she's gone into labor or WHATEVER.

"Much time is wasted (particularly by young ladies) in writing and answering such epistles as are termed letters of friendship—meaning long documents (frequently with crossed lines) filled with regrets at absence, asseverations of eternal affection, modest deprecations of your humble self, and enthusiastic glorifyings of your exalted correspondent; or else wonderments at both of you being so much alike, and so very congenial, and anticipations of rapture at meeting again, and lamentations at the slow progress of time, till the ecstatic hour of re-union shall arrive […] such letters as these are of no manner of use but to foster a sickly, morbid feeling (very often a fictitious one), and to encourage nonsense and destroy all relish for such true friendship as is good and wholesome."

—Pretty sure Miss Leslie has been reading alllll my text messages and thinks I use far too many emojis

when she told me that her Zen-like equanimity did not save her from the Internet obsession trap.

When she left her job in public radio, all her mentors told her that to succeed in freelancing, she needed social media. It would be a network and a megaphone, and it would launch her. They were right, and sure enough, Alexandra turned out to be very, very good at it and amassed thousands of followers (because who doesn't want some yoga-nature walk-Xanax-cupcake in their life?)

But, she said, something was off.

"I noticed myself almost unconsciously checking my phone, checking my stats, seeing who had liked or re-tweeted my posts," she said. "And every time it was this little dopamine drip in my brain: My phone would vibrate and drip, drip, drip, and I could *never* get enough of it."

In a very short time, she'd gone from someone who had lived

several very contented decades without Twitter to someone who found herself reliant on that constant positive attention.

The final straw, she said, was the great and terrible Twitter calculation.

"I looked at the number of times I had tweeted in the past year and multiplied that by approximately how long I would spend on each tweet—thinking about the tweet, composing the tweet, editing the tweet, posting the tweet—," she paused to roll her eyes. "*Then* checking how people were reacting to the tweet.

"And I multiplied that by how many years I had left in my life. And I realized, holy shit, if I carry on this way, I am going to spend *literally years of my life* tweeting. I think it was around 9 years. That stunned me.

"It caused me to think: At the end of my life, when I look at how I spent my time, my contribution to the world, my body of work, will I be proud of that, or will I feel regret? For me—and I know this is not the answer for everyone, but it was for me—the answer was immediately regret."

These days, Alexandra's Internet footprint is much smaller, and she's much happier. After the 9 years' worth of Twitter calculation, she decided that it wasn't worth it, and over the years she's slowly quit almost every bit of social media in favor of in-person conversation and company. Also, for the record, she's booked out until the middle of next year, so her business seems to be doing just fine.

Alex then quoted, "I think a lot of people forget that the Internet is your tool. You can reclaim it and use it or not use it however you want.

"People are *very* fascinated by these choices," she said. "It's like we're in this fog where people forget that not having a Facebook account is an option for you. Nothing is mandatory."

It wasn't until she slowly let go of the various pieces that she saw how much the constant contact had changed her.

"After a couple of months—oh, how would I describe it? It was that there had been a loud refrigerator buzzing in my brain that I had gotten so accustomed to that I didn't know it was there. And finally someone turned it off, and I was like, 'Oh, that's what silence sounds like.' The part of my brain that had been devoted to Twitter was finally quiet, and my brain felt a lot more spacious."

Doesn't that quieted mind thing sound wonderful? You don't have to make it permanent—decide and post that you are on a 2-week or a month-long break. You will continue to exist. You may miss out on a few things, but they are very unlikely to be of essential importance to your life. And who knows what you will notice, achieve, and experience when you're using all of that brain space that's currently taken up with the ever-updating feed.

Alexandra *decided* how to use the Internet to live her life in accordance with her values. So did Sheila and Alex and Lelia. While some of those women are constantly connected and others will go for weeks at a stretch without checking in, the common ground is that their engagement is deliberate and mindful. It is their tool, and they use it to interact with humans kindly and lovingly.

CHAPTER THREE

Grace UNDER FIRE

Sometimes, it's easy to be gracious. When you are in a good mood, when life and the people in it are both pleasing and kind—well, it's not a big lift to smile and ask the librarian how he's doing. Enjoy those times, deposit them in the bank of good and easy karma, practice, and perfect when it's smooth sailing. After all, it's easier to learn to weld when the shop is not on fire.

But here I'll continue the welding metaphor: Grace is steel, not a piñata, 🍍 and it is tested, tempered, and ultimately forged when the world itself seems to be burning to the ground.

A friend of mine once noted that a boat sufficiently far out in the ocean experiences a tsunami as a swell, a sea that rises and then settles. That same boat, if it stays in the harbor, will not exist after that wave arrives.

So now, let us square our shoulders, put on our lipstick (or tinted Burt's Bees lip balm or face paint that makes you look like a zebra or whatever your battle armor of choice is), and turn our faces toward that blistering heat or sky-high wave, knowing that too often, the only way around it is through it.

🍍 Piñatas do *terribly* in fires; even adorable ones have virtually zero coping mechanisms. They are wonderful at parties, not so wonderful while on fire.

Breaking down those tsunami strategies...

Throughout this chapter, I will sometimes suggest one or more of these strategies in the face of difficulty.

1. **Get to Higher Ground:** In doing this, you do not entirely remove yourself from the situation but instead strategically retreat to a place of safety in order to take further action.

2. **Observe from Above:** This is detachment, and sometimes that is the very healthiest thing you can do. For though life is shockingly full of storms, most of them are not aimed at you. Never forget that when that airplane loses pressure,🍍 you put on your own oxygen mask first. Otherwise, you will pass out and then *no one* will get an oxygen mask.

3. **Wade in the Water:** The most terrifying option, and sometimes, the only one. Make sure that your compass is properly oriented, put on your life jacket, and wade into those terrifying and troubled waters.

These strategies won't turn the tsunami around, but they allow you to survive intact and be there to help pick up the pieces.

🍍 As someone who is terrified of flying, I remain convinced that this happens in one out of every three flights, despite mountains of personal and scientific evidence to the contrary.

Life will throw every last thing it can at you, darlings, and I wish it wouldn't, but I promise it will. You don't get to choose what, when, or how the trouble looks, but you *do* get to choose who *you* are through these moments, tiny or enormous.

There is not enough paper in the world to address every situation you could ever come across that will test you. Nor, of course, would I want all of the world's lovely trees* to be wasted on my blathering.

I can, however, roughly categorize challenges into the following:

🐚 Someone is being unkind.

🐚 You must stand up for something you believe in.

🐚 Things do not go the way you thought/wished/assumed/desperately needed them to.

🐚 You are caught in the middle of others' conflicts.

🐚 Someone is leaving your life, or you are leaving theirs.

🐚 The Center Cannot Hold.

Also, since this chapter is kinda heavy, instead of English, I'm going with French, because *petite, moyenne, et énorme* will cheer (at least) me up as I type of moving through sadness, pain, and grief.

Finally, here is a little something I've noticed in my own life, and I'll bet if you look back on your own narrative, you may see, too. *The less I understand why something is happening in the moment, the more understanding and growth will ultimately come to me.*

Unlike tsunamis, conflicts between people almost always have two sides, and you will have an easier time finding a resolution if you take a moment to step back and get more information rather than react defensively by lashing out or beating a total retreat. So pause, pause, PAUSE. Then remember that ole chestnut about non-fatal things making you stronger is emotionally, though not physically or sexually, true.

We don't know what our capacities are until they are tested, and

---

🍍 I once read something that suggested that maybe plants and trees *are* mobile and sentient, but their time lines are drastically different from ours; so what's a year to them might be 100 to us. DID I JUST BLOW YOUR MIND? I casually ask any currently stoned readers.

learning how to approach difficult situations with a sense of calm is an invaluable skill. The ultimate expression of graciousness is being able to use it under pressure when it would be so much easier to fall apart or throw a fit. You'll be amazed at how many situations can be diffused with kindness and compassion when you pause to find objectivity.

For the situations where that doesn't solve the problem? I still recommend bringing those qualities, because, even if they don't solve the situation, they protect you and ensure that when this passes—and it will, everything does, 100 percent of the time to date—you will be able to look back on your own actions without pain or regret. And sometimes in the very shittiest situations, that is the only good thing we can take with us.

All right, then. Off we go.

Someone Is Being Unpleasant, Unkind, or Unfair

The thing that is so very unfortunate about other people, but also the *most sane thing we can realize,* is that we do not control them. No matter how good our counsel or how obviously right our plans are, off they go, on their way, doing things that we may not like or approve of . . . or have even thought possible in the spectrum of human behavior. And it's tempting, in those situations, to assume those people are idiots and write them off for the waste of time, space, and energy that they may occasionally feel like. But if you take a step back and really look at the situation that is causing you such agita, what kind of deliberate injustices against you do you actually see?

"I think the vast majority of rude or offensive behavior is unintentional; it almost always comes from lack of awareness," said Daniel Post Senning, great-great-grandson of etiquette queen Emily Post. "So you can say to yourself—*doesn't that person know better?* And yes, they may know better—just like *you* know better. So just like you know better but make mistakes, they do it, too."

He added that manners and etiquette are really only useful tools for self-measurement, and I'd add that noticing and encouraging best practices in one person (you) is a pretty full-time job.

So what *do* you do?

Petite Catégorie

The Combative: "Eh-hemmmm. Um, excuse me? This pug? This pug is yours? Why is this pug sniffing my dog? It's called 'boundaries,' and I suggest you *and* that snuffling monstrosity look into it."

A stranger is, for reasons that seem entirely unclear, yelling at you. Perhaps it's a high-strung dog owner at the dog park who believes your pug poses a threat to their German shepherd's safety, or someone in traffic who does not realize they *are* traffic, or someone who let go of the end of their rope a while ago and is *not* okay with your standing in line at the candy store.

Suggested Strategy: Observe from Above

"I always try to give others the benefit of the doubt, because you just don't know where they're coming from," Virginia Provosty said. "And that could be where they're coming from in the last 20 minutes or the last 20 years."

Yes, it could be that this person is someone who feels that yelling at strangers is an acceptable and frequent part of their daily routine, *or* it could be that this dog park outing is their break from sitting at the deathbed of their favorite person on earth. You don't know! So if you aren't aware of having deliberately caused injury to the person claiming otherwise, take a deep breath and tell yourself that it's not about you, really.

"A really great habit is to remember that you don't have to answer right away," Virginia said. "Just pause, then look them in the eye, and say, 'I'm sorry you're upset. Is there something I can do to help you?'"

If, she said, this is met with further anger, then you're free to disengage.

"A friend may inadvertently say something that you do not like to hear or may make a remark that is not pleasant to you. Unless it is prefaced with a *previous* apology; or unless she desires you 'not to be offended at what she is going to say;' or unless she informs you that 'she considers it her duty always to speak her mind,' you have no right to suppose the offence premeditated."

—Miss Leslie, on letting people gently know that they hurt your feelings

"Just say, 'I'm sorry, I wish there was something I could do to help,' and walk away."

Moyenne Catégorie

The Resentful: "Oh, you got that promotion? Must be nice to have the boss have a crush on you. No! I mean it, it's nice that you have your own way of getting ahead."

A coworker—perhaps even a boss—is toxic to you for reasons you do not understand. It may be that they're just an abusive person or it may be that this behavior *is* directed at you.

Suggested Strategy: Get to Higher Ground

"If this is someone you work with and their ugly habits are daily, they're extremely unhappy," Virginia said. "This is a time that requires boundaries; you don't want to be in a position where you get hammered every single day."

She suggested that you broach this directly with the person, at a time when they seem more or less relaxed, and don't speculate on *why* or even *what* they're doing, just speak in terms of yourself.

"Don't be afraid to speak the truth with love—'Is there something I can do to improve the relationship between us?' And then, if they say they don't know what you mean, you can say, 'Well, it just seems like much of the time you seem really unhappy when X, Y, or Z happens, and I wanted to see if there was a way I can make that better.'"

Lelia Gowland said that keeping shared goals in sight and not internalizing that toxicity is the best you can hope for.

"When the relationship isn't one that you can salvage, it becomes less about the relationship and more about figuring out how you can engage that gets the work done but prevents the emotional damage from hitting you hard," she said. "And with toxic people, that can be enormously difficult."

Lelia said protecting yourself and your sanity needs to be the top priority.

"Some venting time is important but probably not with coworkers," she said. "It's valuable to have someone unconnected to the situation as an ally and a listening ear."

Énorme Catégorie

The Engima: "Did I sleep with him? Yes, I did. Am I sorry? I think so. Would I do it again? Maybe. Wait, are you *mad* at me?"

You: I think we should talk about this later.

Someone very close to you has acted cruelly or betrayed you in what, perhaps, feels like an unforgivable way. You do not believe they acted in good faith and feel deeply injured by what transpired.

Suggested Strategy: Wade into the Water

Before you cut this person off forever, you want to be *sure* they realize how much they have hurt you and give them a chance to explain themselves.

In some situations, you *don't* have to give them that chance; if even revisiting the subject causes you extreme pain and/or there is no way their actions could be interpreted as anything but atrocious, you may cut them out of your life. Miss Manners advises giving them icy hellos at social occasions, and, if they try to press contact, you may offer a very, very quiet "I don't want anything to do with you, and I'm sure you know why," and then turn away.

(continued on page 74)

Lelia's Top 10 Negotiation Tips

Lelia Gowland is the best and she shared her top 10 tips on gracious negotiations. This is an aces time to remind you that while these examples are about work, they can be useful anywhere, anytime that someone's viewpoint is not aligning with yours, and you'd like to get to consensus within the "us."

1. **Remember the definition of negotiation.** "Discussion aimed at reaching an agreement." That's not that scary, now is it? Negotiation isn't just for salaries and big purchases. You negotiate all the time in your daily life and are probably already pretty darn good at it.

2. **Know your goals.** Before the negotiation, determine what your priorities are. In applying for jobs, a flexible schedule might make your heart sing but maternity leave doesn't matter. Know your "must haves," "like to haves," and "deal breakers" going in; that way, you can be focused on what you want instead of being anchored by their initial offer.

3. **Do your research.** Your request will be stronger with context and precedents. Using salary calculators to find comparable salaries for people with your level of experience allows you to justify your request in terms of market value in the region and ensures you're not lowballing yourself.

4. **Use empathy.** Whether you're talking with your boss, colleague, or client, consider what the situation is like from their perspective. When appropriate, framing your request in terms of how it benefits your counterpart can make it more likely that you get what you want and, bonus, makes them feel like you are considering their perspective.

5. **Practice.** You don't want the first time you say the words out loud to be in a meeting with your boss, which can come with a high risk of word vomit. Role playing with a trusted friend, partner, or advisor can help you figure out what feels comfortable and authentic—and coherent.

6. **Know your counterpart.** Pay attention to the ways your counterpart likes to receive information. Some swear by numbers, while others might prefer a narrative. Whatever it might be, make your request using that language.

7. **Get comfy with silence.** When I'm nervous, I tend to speak more and more quickly—not exactly helpful in a negotiation. Silence makes most people (including your counterpart) uncomfortable. Make your ask and then drop the mic. Count to 20 to give the other person a chance to think and share their perspective.

8. **Listen.** This might seem obvious, but have you ever been so worried about what you're going to say next that you forget to listen to what the other person is saying? If you're listening closely, you can notice what's not being said and determine what additional information you might want.

9. **Ask questions.** Restating your counterpart's perspective using questions like "Did I understand you correctly that _____?" can help avoid misunderstanding and demonstrate that you're invested in their interests.

10. **Follow up.** Don't underestimate the power of a quick thank-you note with the outline of what you discussed. This is an opportunity to make them feel valued and clarify that you're both on the same page moving forward.

But! Let's say you're giving them a shot at salvaging things. You say, "So-and-so, it really broke my heart that you _____. I am so deeply hurt. Why did you do that?"

They may offer up a truly reasonable explanation that you just had not thought of.

They may offer up an excuse, which is different from an explanation, and you are entitled to think it's self-serving bullshit meant to assuage their own guilt. You may also resent any attempts they may make to try to force you to forgive them.

Here, it is useful to note that a very large percentage of apologies are not true expressions of regret meant to heal another person, but rather a way of asking for our own absolution via rehashing and reinflicting the wound—on the wounded. Let's never make that second kind of apology, and when we are offered those apologies, say something neutral—"I appreciate that," without saying you forgive them.

Now the ball is in your court. A few options:

- You can forgive them (or not) and resume relations.

- You can forgive them (or not) and *not* resume relations.

- You can forgive them and not resume relations *at the moment.*

Just because an apology is offered does not mean that you must respond with immediate forgiveness; to forgive something means to truly set it down and move forward without that particular pain. If you're not there yet, it doesn't mean you'll never be—but you don't have to pretend that you are right now. "I forgive you" are powerful and important words, right up there with "I love you," and shouldn't be offered unless they are meant.

You can say, "It's okay," which gives that person the knowledge that whatever they have done hasn't ruined your life. You can say, "I appreciate your saying that," which acknowledges receipt of the emotion, essentially, though doesn't speak to where *you* are. "Thank you" is also a useful phrase if you are genuinely grateful for their seeing the error but are not yet ready to let it go.

You Must Stand Up for Yourself and/or for Goodness, Generally

Petite Catégorie

The Crude: "Oh, yeah, I just grab them by the [genitalia]. Do it all the time! They *like* it."

What's that you say, fellow human? You're telling a hilarious[*] rape joke? Or a racist one? Or a discourse on how trans people are, as you put it, "faking it," an elaborate long con to get into a public restroom . . . why? Or *any* cruel, thoughtless, kick-down thing that is on your mind?

You can go one of two ways with this, depending on your level of contact with this person and how offensive what they have said is. If this is a one-off, a person at a party you don't know and don't care to know, then your best bet may be to Observe from Above—you cannot save everyone.

Strategy: Observe from Above

Ah, what a pity it is that so many humans choose to make the WORST mouth noises! But they do. And who could ever say why?

If you were so inclined, you could spend *every moment of the rest of your life* ferreting out upsetting things other people have said and then reacting with hurt, anger, or even hatred. That is one option on the table.

A *better* option, however, is to remember that most people don't need to play roles in your life and, as discussed in the Internet chapter, if what they are saying isn't useful to you, then you don't have to listen. Nor do you have to educate them. That last one is so, so tempting. But again, what do you want to do with your limited time—try to explain the intricacies of privilege and oppression to someone who is *not* receptive to that, or focus your energies in

[*] It is never hilarious.

places that it might actually make a difference in addressing those issues? Save the angry energy for working toward the world you want—not needlessly upsetting yourself at a party.

So. This person said something terrible. Let's go ahead and *make a teeny sucking air through your teeth noise,* pause, assume a puzzled and slightly dismayed expression, then say, "Hmmm. *Anyway,*" and here, you may note that you are going to excuse yourself, then do so without saying it was a pleasure to meet or see them. Just opt right out!

If physical departure is not an option, then go for a social and emotional departure from this icky place that they have taken everyone in earshot.

"Hmmmm. *Anyway,* Laura! How are your quails doing? Have the new chicks hatched yet?"

Strategy: Wade in the Water

Perhaps this person is unavoidable—a relative or coworker or friend's significant other or even (please, Lord, no!) a boss. You see them again and again and will for the foreseeable future.

While, again, what other people say and think isn't up to you and you can't hope to change them, you *can* make clear that you are not the right audience for this intolerance, bigotry, or whatever idiot sentiment, and you will do this by putting them on the spot.

> *Coworker's Ugly Punchline:* And that's why you NEVER invite the Senegalese to an infant's birthday party!
>
> *You,* with a puzzled expression: I don't get it.
>
> *Coworker:* (Tries to explain joke)
>
> *You:* Huh? Why . . . why would you say that?
>
> *Coworker:* (Makes mouth noises)
>
> *You:* Well, that's an interesting point of view.

Let this hang. The idea here is to induce discomfort in the other human, to give no feedback either positive or negative that would show you either appreciate it or that they have succeeded in offend-

"Should you chance to be thrown into the presence of persons who have proved themselves your enemies, and with whom you can have no intercourse, say nothing either *to* them or *at* them, and do not place yourself in their vicinity. To talk *at* a person is mean and vulgar. Those who do it are fully capable of writing anonymous and insulting letters, and they often do so."

—Miss Leslie, on how to properly ice someone out

ing you. Just ask them to be accountable for what they just said.

If this person is a True Believer in whatever they are espousing, and it's not so much offensive remarks (though there are plenty of those) but an evangelical zeal to convince you that raw quinoa is the source of all truth and light, you can disengage, again and again, forever.

"I know we have very different views on this."

"I don't have much to say about XYZ and would prefer to chat about (*anything but* XYZ)."

"I know you feel that way, Uncle So-and-so."

If you're not going to be convinced, and you're not, then just loop through those three lines until they tucker themselves out. You may have to do this for *years*. But when you say, "I disagree," that opens the door for the other person to try to convince you *and the conversation will only get harder to leave.*

Moyenne Catégorie

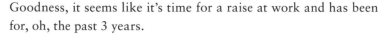

The Thoughtless: "Hey, So-and-so? I've got a great opportunity for you! Basically, you're going to do all the work of a director, except with your current salary! And no power or input! We are all so proud of you."

Goodness, it seems like it's time for a raise at work and has been for, oh, the past 3 years.

Here, let us return to Lelia, whose job, basically, is coaching women on negotiating.

"Women are constantly told that they're bad at negotiating, and I think that's bullshit," she said. "A lot of the ways that many women are socialized to handle themselves are actually *really, really good* negotiation strategies."

Go onnnnnn, Lelia!

"If you think about effective negotiations—listening, asking questions, using empathy, demonstrating concern for another's well-being—well, those are the quote-unquote feminine characteristics," she said.

Before you negotiate, Lelia said, you need to get clear on what you are advocating for. It is usually not just about getting this much more money, but rather a question of power, work environment, personal freedom, recognition and, yes, money, too.

"I had a client who was really stressed because she'd been at a job for 30 years and hadn't gotten a sizable raise in some time. *Plus,* unfortunately, she wasn't in a great position to negotiate for that raise. But when we talked through it, her actual desires were about being valued and acknowledged for the work she'd done, and while she didn't get a raise, she did get a sizable bonus and that recognition. She could've looked at it as a failure, but instead she assessed what her priorities were and then worked to meet those needs."

And a no isn't necessarily no, but it *does* require follow-up questions.

"If I want to work from home on Fridays, and I say, 'Hey, Kelly, can I work from home on Fridays?' and you say no, asking follow-up questions is more likely to get the result I want. Ask about the reasoning behind the no. Is it possible to work from home another day because there's an important meeting on Fridays? Is it a no-right-now-but-yes-in-6-months? Is it a no, never because this office culture requires everyone's presence full-time?

"In any negotiation, framing the request in the interest of the other party can be effective," Lelia said. "So, perhaps, 'Hey, Kelly,

I know we've got this report that we need to do every month, and we're struggling to get it out on time. In the office, there are so many projects and conversations that pull my attention away. Would you be open to my working from home on Fridays to ensure that report gets knocked out and we have more time to go back and forth on it in advance of the deadline?"

You shouldn't ever be disingenuous, Lelia said, but added that while your original motivation to work from home may have nothing to do with that report and *everything* to do with staying cozy in your alligator onesie pajamas, you should still look at every request through the lens of the other person's needs and desires and figure out a way to make a pitch that gets both of you what you want.

Finally, she suggests that anyone asking for a raise remember that they need to price and value themselves fairly—going to a salary calculator like Payscale.com or Salary.com is an important first step to figuring out what someone in your position and location should be making.

Things Are Not Going Your Way

Pop quiz, hotshot: Which sea is the worst sea? Answer: the Gulf Between How You Think Life Should Be versus How It Actually Is.

This gulf contains so many things, big and small—what you want your job to be versus what it is. What you want a certain person to be like versus who they are—and yes, that person may well be you.

Our wishes and desires . . . well, we sometimes get them! But so often we do not, and even if we *do* get what we wished for, well, as pretty much everybody knows (or has seen in a movie), it doesn't make us feel the way we were hoping it would.

A good bit of strategy here is to let go of expectations you have that you *know* will never be met. If your boss has never given you a scrap of evidence that he or she intends to promote you, why

To be fair, this is a trick question because it's a gulf, not a sea, and also you did not guess correctly because I made up the answer.

stubbornly cling to the idea that somehow that will change rather than, y'know, trying to get around them and/or get a new job? Passively wishing for things to be different and complaining about how unfair it is that they're not wastes those most precious and nonrenewable resources, energy and time.

A GOOD WAY TO SAY THE RIGHT THING WHEN STAKES ARE HIGH...

One of the most life-altering (really, social interaction-altering) pieces I've ever read is "How Not to Say the Wrong Thing," by Susan Silk and Barry Goldman, published in the *Los Angeles Times* on April 7, 2013. Please read it if you haven't—it's that good and important.

Susan, who is a breast cancer survivor, noticed something upsetting as she was struggling with the illness: A lot of her friends wanted to complain *to her* about how *her* cancer impacted *their* lives.

We've probably all experienced shades of this—when you're already emotionally and/or physically exhausted by something, yet someone who is *less* affected than you wants you to make them feel better about your problems.

So Susan came up with the Ring Theory.

"It works for all kinds of crises: medical, legal, financial, romantic, even existential," the couple wrote.

Here's how it works: Envision tree rings; everyone who is impacted is in one of those rings. There is one person who is *most* affected by this; if the problem at hand is Susan's cancer, then obviously that person is Susan. She is in the center. The next larger ring contains maybe her husband and children. The ring around that one contains family members and maybe the closest friends; the next one, friends, and so on outward.

This, Susan and Barry write, is the Kvetching Order. The person in the center can complain to anyone, at any time! However, those elsewhere can only complain to those people in larger rings (read: less close to the trauma) than they are.

Petite Catégorie

The Enigma: "Well, you know . . . *[lowers voice]* if you ask me, the *real* problem with the city parks department is that it's in the pocket of the Israeli lobby."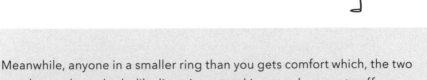

Meanwhile, anyone in a smaller ring than you gets comfort which, the two note, almost always looks like listening or making good, concrete offers, and almost never includes unsolicited advice or complaining about their problem.

This theory is just beautiful and perfect in so many ways, and it has many applications.

It can also be applied to understanding experiences that are different from yours.

Just as I cannot speak authoritatively to what it means to, say, grow up in Switzerland, run my own small business, or lose an immediate family member to cancer, I cannot speak to what it means to be black—or gay or transgender or a person of color or anyone who is not me.

So when people whose voices were often squelched in the past are speaking up, just listen (this means reading and research, not—please, never this—putting someone on the spot and asking them to speak for an entire group).

It's important not to ask for validation that you are one of the okay ones from members of marginalized groups. If you want to be one of the okay ones, listen carefully, then, when you do want to speak, speak outward. If you are white and another white person says something racist, you can quietly point that out, or even just ask what they mean by that. If you are not LGBTQ, you can still state your support, not to those in smaller circles, but to your elected officials and institutions in larger circles.

A very small example: When I was getting . . . unmarried, I knew that lots of my friends and family members would have their feelings about it, and they were totally and completely entitled to those feelings. However, there were a few months when my priority had to be my own feelings, not theirs, and I was not the best person to come to for comfort.

There is something—person, place, or thing—nearby that you absolutely loathe and cannot escape. Perhaps it's Midtown Manhattan, or an elderly crusty-eyed dog and you're allergic, or a person in whom you see no redeeming qualities.

Strategy: Wade in the Water (of Your Own Discomfort)

Pause. Acknowledge your dislike and discomfort with the situation at hand. It's rough, it's unpleasant, it's no fun at all, and maybe it's totally unfair. Then ask yourself the only important question that actually matters—so what?

Midtown Manhattan is a nightmarescape populated entirely by Citi Bike–riding bros shouting about finance. And your feet are cold. And damp. *All* of you is cold and damp. But you have to be here for 3 more hours. And you don't like it.

So what? You're there for a reason, so do what you need to do well and then you can leave.

That dog—which only moments ago was performing tender oral acts on *another* elderly crusty dog—now wants nothing more in the world than to lick your feet, and you are wearing open-toed shoes.

This is disgusting. But so what? Wash your feet after. You'll survive.

This monster of a human being lives on the same planet as your sainted grandmother, breathes the same air, has the absolute *audacity* to continue existing in your social sphere despite your reasonable and well-supported views that they should be set adrift on a garbage barge.

Well, maybe they *should* be on a garbage barge, but there are none in this apartment right now. Even if they were, garbage-barge banishments are outside your scope of power. ﹡ So they're here. You will be in their presence, at least for now. So what? This time will pass, you will leave this room, and we will all, sooner or later, be free.

﹡ For now . . .

Énorme Catégorie

There are things—big things—that you want and expect for yourself that have not happened. Maybe you wish you were in a wonderful marriage with kids. Maybe you wish that you felt valued, appreciated, and heard by the people in your life rather than misunderstood and underappreciated. Maybe you wish you were in a world in which your mom was still alive.

Suggested Strategy: Observe from Above

View from above, then triage, always keeping in mind what is and is not up to you.

What is not up to you:

- Whether you meet the "right" person in a certain month, year, or decade

- Whether you can have biological children

- When people die

- Whether another person behaves the way you wish they would

What is up to you:

- Whether you spend a large portion of your time lamenting what you do not yet have instead of working to make a life that you enjoy and is full of loving people

- Whether you give yourself time to grieve, whether that loss is of a person or the idea of what you thought your life was going to be

- Whether you reach out to people who love you when you need help and let them help you

- Whether you *accept and allow* someone to be cruel to you on an ongoing basis

- Whether you accept without judgment anything you may feel, refrain from having feelings about those feelings, and then . . .

- Whether you choose to stay in the present rather than always fly backward into regret or forward into fear, plus . . .

- Making the conscious choice, again and again, to turn your attention toward gratitude and grace

You Are Caught in the Middle
Moyenne Catégorie

The Meddler: "So then Kyle *gave* Scott the *biggest* hug. It wasn't a *regular* hug, it was like, a *huuuuuuug*. So I looked around to see if Kim had seen it, because it's like, hello, this is your *boyfriend*, are you down with him being *hugged* like *that* by Kyle?"

Alas, two of your very oldest and dearest friends, who were, until last week, equally dear to each other, are having some terrible, ugly, potentially friendship-fatal conflict.

You will probably have your own thoughts on who is right and who is wrong but, barring clear bad faith actions on the part of one (you do not need to be neutral when a friend has done something deliberately or unavoidably cruel to the other※), you will want to . . .

Suggested Strategy: Observe from Above

Just listen. That's all you need to do. Just listen to each of them, saying, "I'm so sorry. That sounds very painful." Let them rail or

---

※ In this situation, you can truthfully say, "Susan, I love you and I don't want to be in the middle, but I think you owe Maria an apology." If they try to argue their case, just reinforce your pro-apology stance, then say that you're not the right person to talk to about this.

If it is a legitimately terrible thing they did, you can be angry on your friend's behalf. You can even perhaps question whether you *want* a friend in your life who does such things. You get to decide.

say whatever they need to say. Sometimes they may need to say the same thing many times as they figure out their understanding and takeaway from the situation.

If and when it seems like the conversation is veering into especially personal, ugly territory (read: you feel guilty for hearing these things about your friend and not sticking up for them), then you can say . . .

"I know you're really angry, and I would be, too. But I love Susan, too, so maybe I'm not the best person to talk to about this."

Do *not* ferry messages from one to the other. That is just asking for complications. Nor is it your job to play peacemaker; you are not the UN.

Remember that whatever happened happened *between them*, and you will never get an entirely objective account. Nor would it matter even if you had one; the only people who can truly sort through this situation are the two people in conflict with each other. The more emotion is involved, the further we move from the story of what actually happened and more into the narrative of our hearts. That narrative is what's driving this, and people do not need to prove their feelings are valid. They just feel them, and you can offer comfort in whatever way you see fit.

This advice, in fact, can extend to *any* similar situation, whether it's a spat between coworkers or a divorce in your immediate family that leaves everyone devastated.

Frankie Bell🍍 is a lioness of a woman who has been called the most powerful woman in Oregon politics despite never having been elected to office. Her power is soft and *so* vast. It comes from

🍍 Frankie, among other things, has been called the fourth branch of Oregon state government. Also, when I first called her to see if we could get together for an interview, she said, "Listen, kiddo, I'd love to help you with your project but I'm just about to head to Amsterdam. Me and some friends rented a barge and we're going to float around for a week or two."

How many friends, Frankie? "Oh, a whole bunch, it's a good crowd. Nineteen, I think."

How do you decide who gets an invite to this amazing barge party? "Well, I like go-along-to-get-along types, plus people who can kick up their heels *but* don't drink too much and act like fools."

Y'all, all I want in this life is to become Frankie. She is my life goal.

"I have a friend who was in prison for a long time for a violent felony. And he said to me, 'Imagine if, for the rest of your life, everyone's perception of you and every detail boiled down to the one worst day of your life, the most horrible moment, the worst thing you ever did, and that's *it*, that's all you are.'"

—Lelia Gowland, on what compassion looks like

knowing, and being friends, with *everyone in that world*.

Her advice on how to be good to people was the simplest and the best.

"It's just being there, *always* being there. Not being bothered by being awakened in the middle of the night to talk about what's bugging them or to allow them to come and sleep on the davenport or whatever they need," she advised.

From her five decades of watching political spats, large and small, play out through the Oregon capitol, she said she's learned that there are always two sides, and yet you can extend courtesy and attention to everyone.

"I think it's merely listening, and listening hard. And trying not to give advice unless it's asked for," she said. "Really, what people need is—'I get it. I hear you.' And, even if you haven't been through something, conveying that you have a sense of what they're going through and giving empathy. That doesn't mean you have to agree with them."

The Center Cannot Hold, But You Can

Life is hard sometimes, and we all face adverse circumstances that we really, really wish we didn't have to. But even when it's hard to imagine what the other side of a situation or crisis looks like, remember that you will get there by taking things one step at a time. Also remember that the only thing you ultimately have control over in this crazy world is yourself, and no matter how bad things get, you will serve yourself best by being gentle, kind, and patient—with those around you and most of all with yourself. Remember when you feel like you're in the heart of a storm that your perspective might get skewed for the worst, and it's important to take a step back and carefully evaluate each step to make sure that you're truly moving down the best possible path. Remember, too, that you likely have people around you who want to help but may not know the best way to do that, so you shouldn't hesitate to ask if you know what you need. And finally, remember that you are strong, that you are capable, and that the world can be a magical place—even in the worst possible circumstances, you can find joy and serenity if you care to look for it. That is what graciousness is really about.

Let us end with advice from two women who have endured unimaginable things and both emerged as luminous, joyful individuals. This happened because both of them made—and continue to make every day—the choice to walk in grace and, when they couldn't summon it for themselves, allowed others to shower them with grace.

Sheila Hamilton

Only 6 weeks after being formally diagnosed with bipolar II disorder, Sheila's husband committed suicide, leaving her and her 9-year-old daughter, Sophie, with no explanation or note and hundreds of thousands of dollars' worth of debt.

> *Probably the final 6 weeks of my husband's life, it felt like the center couldn't hold. [After being diagnosed with bipolar II disorder and institutionalized], he ended up not being able to respond to any medication, and that was the point at which I felt like everything was crumbling.*
>
> *We want to rely on an institution or other people to fix our problems, and we assume they can. When I realized the*

medical world didn't know how to fix his problem, it felt like everything was crumbling underneath me.

Then something pretty profound happened when I experienced my first panic attack. I couldn't breathe; I thought I was having a heart attack. I just said, "If I can take this one breath, then maybe I can take the next breath."

I began to focus on just living moment by moment to move through the crisis, meaning that the past has already happened; I couldn't do anything about the future in front of me—it was just my fear and conjecture talking. What I found was to be really present in terms of the crisis—what is happening in this moment? And can you handle it right now?

The combination of being able to temper your own anxiety and fear and being willing to ask for help is a pretty good plan.

I was pretty compartmentalized and protective of my husband's personal story and our personal story. My mom had an inkling that something was wrong, but most of my friends had no idea. After he was hospitalized, I had to tell people.

The first thing they say is "What can I do?" And I would actually tell them, "I need you to pick Sophie up after daycare, I need you to walk my dog, or can you come over and have some tea and just keep me company?"

There's a defensiveness that causes us not to ask for help, because we don't want to be seen as vulnerable. But one of the most beautiful things you can do is to allow someone to help you. Before it happened, I valued my privacy and wanted to handle it on my own, but once I realized I was in over my head, I was pretty open about it.

When we try to pretend that we don't have issues, that we don't need help, that we can do it all on our own, we become very robotic and unhuman to the people around us.

It was the first cracking of my shell that needed cracking for a long, long time.

I think maybe the purpose of being human is to integrate fully with yourself, to learn self-love, and to learn how to nurture yourself. Sometimes you can't begin to really understand what's possible in terms of your own personal growth until you've experienced the flip side of that.

I developed this acronym for myself during that time, and the acronym is ARGH, and I still do it every morning when I wake up.

Acceptance: Accept where you are and what's ahead of you, whatever it is.

Resilience: You choose to be resilient, you choose to show your strengths.

Gratitude: For people around you, for everything.

Happiness: Happiness is a choice.

It's a small moment of meditation in which you realize that you are separate from your thoughts and that you can shape them.

So much of our suffering comes from the stories we tell ourselves. I'm a bad wife, I failed my husband. I'm a bad mother, I failed my child. But instead, I say that I did my best. I loved him as much as I could.

Mary Nixon Johnson

I was delighted to see Ms. Mary still behind the counter of an uptown Rite Aid in New Orleans. I remembered her from my college years, how charming and joyful she always seemed, and on a whim, I asked for an interview, from which I emerged changed.

In a book full of admirable and astonishing people, she is singular

and stands in a place beyond my comprehension. Mary is graciousness embodied, and she radiates that kindness to everyone who
walks through that door, to everyone at her church, to everyone she
meets. She chooses, every day, to turn her face always toward the sun,
toward goodness. She has every valid reason a human can have not
to make this choice, and yet she always does.

*Just touch somebody with your goodness and your
mercy. Touch somebody with your gifts, as you pass,
because you may never pass that way again. Give them
something beautiful, something to think about.*

*I got married at 24 and it was 10 years before I got preg-
nant. I prayed so hard, every day. I prayed that the Lord
would let me get pregnant.*

*When I got pregnant, I carried that baby so well, no
swollen feet—nothing! When I did get to the hospital, it
wasn't about 2 hours until that boy was born. That was my
first child, Lovie, born in 1971, and the next thing I know,
1972, I got pregnant again, another boy. That was John
John. In 1975, I had another boy, Too Too.*

*My husband said, "We can't be supporting all these
kids," so they tied my tubes.*

*I asked [God] for one thing, and he gave me a whole lot
more. I had a miscarriage, then I had three beautiful boys,
and He let me keep them for 6 years and enjoy them. Then
He took them home.*

While driving drunk, her husband was in an accident and all three
of her sons were killed instantly.

*I had all three of the little coffins around the altar and I
just—it was something. It was overwhelming. My people
came from North Carolina but they didn't know what to
do, so I had to pick out all the little outfits.*

When my kids were killed, I didn't want to live. I just wanted to die. And my sister came and spent a week or so with me and she was sitting in my house, and I wasn't talking, wasn't doing nothing, and she said, "What's the matter with you?" and I said, "I'm waiting to die. The Lord took my kids and now he can take me; I'll wait."

And one day after another was coming in, and I wasn't dying, I'm just sitting there. And the doctor goes, "Girl, what's the matter with you? You're not gonna die, so you may as well get up and live."

I buried them on Tuesday and went to church on Sunday. That's where I get my peace. But I walked through that door and I was angry.

I said to God, "I did all that and I can't do no more so you take me. I've done all I could and I couldn't fix it; my husband's still acting stupid, I couldn't deal with him either, so just take it, just take [all the anger] from me." And He did.

One day, it was early in the morning, I got out of my house and walked down the fence, and I'm standing by the neighbors' fence and something was coming up out of me. I was so happy! I'm happy! I was just happy!

And I said to myself, "Girl, what's the matter with you? You lost everything you have, and now you're out here being happy?"

Mary and her husband evacuated during Hurricane Katrina and returned to devastation. Shortly after that, her husband was killed by a neighbor.

It was the 4th of July and we had a barbecue, and he was taking the food up to them. I told him before he left, "Don't go up there," but he took his behind up there and he never came back.

No one was ever convicted, no, because he was in the house.

After that, I'd walk on the other side of the street from their house. I wouldn't speak to them for 2 years.

And one day I passed by and I spoke to my neighbor, and he was so shocked. And he said to the whole neighborhood, "Ms. Mary spoke to me. Finally, I can sleep at night again."

[College students] come in the store and they're just sad, it's raining, or it's storming—it's a "bad day," and I have to tell them it's not a bad day. Just enjoy what's in the present because you can't change anything. So why waste your time being concerned with what happened in the past?

I just try to appreciate each day, each moment that I live. Every person I see, it's the chance to see the good in them, the God in them, and perhaps show them the God in me.

We are supposed to work together and come together, that's what we're made for. We need each other, we do, we need each other. But you need to be fine on your own, too. I am! I look at myself and think, "I'm fine." I have peace, joy, and contentment.

I've been through the fire and I've been through the storm, and I'm still here.

If you do all you can do, I don't care what you've got to go through, you can stand it. You might not like it, but you can get through it, if you're doing your part.

Let us go forth into the world now, gathering all our fortitude, all our kindness, never forgetting the power of our choices. Let's be as

Mary-like as possible. For while she has a singular and powerful alchemy that burnishes her pain into joy, every one of us has shades and fractions of that same capacity, and we must use it.

This world has quite enough pain, and who couldn't use a bit more joy?

CHAPTER FOUR

How to be Gracious to yourself

Okay, y'all? Real quick? Can we talk about somebody? Someone who is the *worst*?

There is no end to the flaws you can find with this individual. And I'll bet you're always open to mentioning these weaknesses. Loudly. Clearly. Repeatedly. Every day! Every damn day, you *remind* this person of their vast failings. Sometimes multiple times per day—you are just trying to help, after all.

You probably whisper to them, "You will never be the person you want to be. Only an *idiot*—an *idiot-stick*, really—would say that thing you just said. Oh my GOD, everything out of your MOUTH today is the verbal equivalent of that coffee stain on your blouse. Which, of COURSE, your blouse is stained. Stains would be a *great* nickname for you, Stains von Schlumpadump.

"Also, just a few really quick reminders: Your ribs are fat, your nose is stupid, your career is a fluke of your having tricked everyone, and *any minute now* they will catch on and you'll be publically shamed on the Internet. Also, when you wear flat shoes you walk like an arthritic duck."

You spend a great deal of mental energy trying to divine what *others* think of this person, which is even *more* important than what you think of them. You stealthily guide conversations toward this topic, always gathering clues. You latch onto every offhanded comment and hastily issued invitations, trying to catch a glimpse of . . . well, the inside of other people's minds. Well, at least their thoughts pertaining to this individual.

To be clear: This person's comfort, serenity, and needs *always* come last. Except, sometimes, when their comfort, serenity, and needs are the *only* ones that exist in the world.

Hover a hand slightly over your collarbone; your pearls are about to get clutched as they've never been clutched before: *Bruce Willis was dead the* entire *time, Snape turns out to be* good *after all, and yes, obviously, the person in question is* you.

Or maybe it used to be you, and you are trying to get better. Maybe there are some parts that sound exactly right and others that sound completely insane, because, of course, I can only speak to *my* internal dialogue. Though I really do look forward to the day when science can make those thoughts audible. (IF AND ONLY IF you consented, because, come on, that would be *most* fascinating, and also I would really, really like to hear my dog's internal monologue.)

Graciousness is about kindness and generosity to humans; since you are a human, you should therefore reap the benefits of being treated well by yourself and be able to accept the kindness offered to you by others without trying to talk them out of it.

If this isn't convincing, perhaps this will be: True graciousness, and the comfort and generosity that comes with it, begins with feeling at home in your own skin.

Think of it this way, darling and priceless melons: These nasty trains of thoughts, these critiques and moments of self-abuse, make it *very hard* to approach the world and our own actions effectively. It's very hard to feel comfortable in a room when somebody is berating your every gesture, and when that somebody is living in your head (it's coming from *inside the house!*), it can feel like there's no place in the world to relax and experience a bit of peace. So for the next few pages, let's focus on the hows and whys of turning the volume down on those nasty, repetitive, boring, and, let's face it, self-indulgent voices so that we can be happier and more effective in our own skin.

"The heart of graciousness, for me, is that it's someone who appears to be at ease," said Daniel Post Senning, great-great-grandson of etiquette queen Emily Post. "It's that quality and having the ability to put *others* at ease, and I think your ability to make other people feel comfortable is dependent on your ability to feel at ease with yourself.

"Someone gracious—they seem integrated," Daniel continued. "What they're doing makes sense, it's connected, and it gives *us* a sense of ease . . . when a person has that quality, it's almost impossible [to miss]—being at ease in your own body, at ease with your own emotions . . . that becomes the foundation to gracious behavior.

"Self-acceptance translates into almost any situation. So often, in etiquette, we talk about how accidents *will* happen, mistakes *will* be made, and how you handle that says so much."

If you wouldn't mind joining me on an imaginary trip, then please hop aboard the Convenient Fictional Anecdote Express! Picture a dinner party—no, two of them, happening side by side, like 1998's *Sliding Doors.*

Left Side: The host opens the door and is delighted to see you, even though you're half an hour early (oops! no traffic!). There is a smudge of flour on their face but they smile wide, say they are happy to see you, and ask if you'd like to hand them your coat. Then they tell you to go ahead and flop on the couch, if you like, and please have some of this cheese that they're about to put out. The host is not pressed that you are early; they seem, in fact, quite pleased that their friends are in close proximity and also . . . Cheese! Hooray, the party's begun!

Right Side: As you are knocking, you hear annoyed voices inside—Host One is NOT happy with the fact that Host Two has been doing WHATEVER while Host One has SLAVED AWAY, and now the guests are HERE and this place still LOOKS LIKE IT HAS BEEN HIT BY A HOT LIQUID GARBAGE TORNADO. A long pause. The door opens and Host One has a tight-lipped smile on, closed lips taut against teeth. "Hiiiiiiiii, oh my God, I'm so sorry, I know it smells like a wharf covered in chronically ill sea lions in here, it's just horrible, I feel awful that you even have to see this, please let me pay all PTSD-related therapy bills, UGH! Come in. There's cheese over there, but it's . . . ugh . . . well, I asked Host Two to get Fancy Delicious cheese and he came back with this horrific substance that brings shame to the good name of cheese every-

---

I really did not mean to make this chapter a celebration of the late '90s American movie canon, but, you know, here we are and it feels right. In case I can't cram it in elsewhere, 1999's *Mystery Men* was *criminally* underrated and the only movie mentioned in this chapter whose release date I did not have to look up on IMDB.

where, so know it's going to be *awful,* but please go ahead and have some. If you want."

Which party is going to be fun? Which party is going to be an exhausting evening of reassuring someone that their house does *not* smell like a wharf, that the recipe they stupidly chose is delicious even though it's not what they expected, that you *love* everything because anything less isn't strong enough to cut through their certainty that everything they do is horrifying?

At a party, the host sets the tone. Any guest would have to be one cool customer☙ not to be affected by someone radiating stress at their own failings in everything they have tried to do for you.

Lovely reader, you are the host of your own life, and everyone in it is going to have a lot more fun if you can relax a little bit and enjoy yourself.

In order to make others feel comfortable and loved, you must feel comfortable and loved. It matters less whether you keep a perfect house or serve the perfect hors d'oeuvres than it does that you set a tone of welcoming acceptance in (and of) your own life. This is what separates graciousness from compulsive people-pleasing, which, in the end, almost never works and is a swift path to madness.

So if you, like so many of us, equate treating yourself kindly to selfishness, then for now, just remember that treating yourself well is good for everyone.

Graciousness toward others starts with what we say, and how we say it, and then listening carefully. Graciousness to yourself is no different.

Spend a day just listening to your internal monologue. If it helps, and there is no one around you (or they're super cool and you explain ahead of time what you're doing), say it out loud. Every thought you have about yourself.

Why aren't you doing your work? You are so lazy.

Oh, you have a UTI? Wah wah, no one cares.

(continued on page 102)

☙ Historical examples of cool customers: Oprah Winfrey, Winston Churchill, Werner Herzog, probably some others I'm forgetting

SEVEN SABOTEURS

THE Thoughtless You

(Forgets an important appointment, then immediately transmogrifies into a Self-Berating You)

You: *Yeah, Brain! I feel bad about that, too. I'm going to take XYZ action and apologize right now. Doing those things now. Done. I've done what I can do, and we need to move on, because the rest of the world has.*

THE Crude You

(Whatever nasty thought about a group of people you don't belong to that embarrasses you as you think it)

You: *Thanks, Brain. That's not true, and I have enough of a job worrying about myself. I'll let this very large gaggle of bachelorette party ladies continue to shriek their way through this hotel lobby because, as Salt-N-Pepa would say, it's none of my business.*

THE Resentful You

Ugh. Why does *that* person appear to have, from the outside, some experience, emotion, life happening, and/or pretty bracelet that *you* want? YOU deserve it, not them. Ugh.

You: *Cool. Good input. Let's pause and remember that comparison is the thief of joy. Instead of throwing my emotional energy into that particular sinkhole, I will turn my thoughts to five things that I'm grateful to have in my life.*

THE Enigma You

Hiiiiiiiiiiiii, I know you're practicing that work presentation, but I have a pretty pressing concern. Have you ever worried about a *Freaky Friday* kind of situation while you're watching the Olympics and someone is about to do the high dive or the ski jump or the uneven bars or something that you *would absolutely kill yourself if you were trying*, and as you're watching, all of a sudden YOUR soul and mind trade place with the athlete's and then your options are either to step off the diving board and ruin forever this person's career they've been working on since they were children OR to go ahead with it and STILL ruin their career with a terrible and dangerous performance? I'm worried that might happen, and I just want to be prepared.

You: *Noted, Brain.*

The Self-Absorbed You

(Basically every thought we ever have about ourselves, whether nice or mean or whatever)

You: *Huh. That's a thought about me, all right! Now, back to living in the actual world.*

Note: *You will have to repeat this over and over and over again almost as long as you're alive. But it's maybe the most important.*

The Meddler You

If *only* this person would do EXACTLY WHAT I WANTED THEM TO DO, then life would be great! Let's seeeeeeee, so I want them to do X, but I don't want them to *know* I'm wanting them to do X, but maaaaaybe if I go ahead and say Y to Z person, then it will get back to them, and *then—*

You: *YO. YOU CAN'T CONTROL OTHER PEOPLE. WORK ON YOURSELF; THAT'S A FULL-TIME JOB, K?*

The Combative You

HOW COULD YOU HAVE POSSIBLY DONE THAT? Oh my GOD, WHY would you DO THAT? You are a MONSTER. You should be cast down into a GODDAMN LABYRINTH so that your HIDEOUS SELF can never, ever, EVER inflict this kind of HORRIBLE PAIN on others. You should probably go burn yourself at the stake.

You: *Huh. This feels like a little too much punishment for the faux pas of having a tiny spot of ketchup on my mouth for 45 seconds. But, as always, thank you for that.*

You're sad about *this?* The same thing you've been sad about for *months?* Pathetic.

Would you say these things to a dear friend? Would you say them to a coworker? Would you say them to someone you *absolutely loathed?*

I sincerely hope not, because that would be cruel and completely unacceptable as a form of human interaction. Here, I will pause to remind you that you are, in fact, a human.

Self-abuse is still abuse.

My friend Jo once told me something that I still think about, something that feels like it takes complete audacity to even *attempt,* but I wish I would.

We were talking with a few other friends about the ways we hurt ourselves. She said that for the past 5 years, she has been working on treating herself like her soulmate. She tries to make decisions for herself out of love, never fear or pride; that even when she doesn't feel like it, she works hard to bestow upon herself the affection, goodwill, and support that she would her own beloved.

You will always be with yourself. You will change and learn and grow but will never be someone other than who you are. You are your own Wilson, Tom Hanks's sole companion in 2000's survival epic *Cast Away.*

Like every other human being on the planet, there are fantastic and wonderful things about you, and there are things you can work on. But as long as you're doing your best—and most of us are at least trying, most of the time—then you should think about cutting yourself some slack when things don't go exactly as you hoped they would. It is about as useful as expecting, through the magical power of self-doubt, that you will wake up one day able to fly.

"It's not possible to be a patient, compassionate, nonjudgmental person who treats other people that way if you're not able to muster that up for yourself," said Holly B. Rogers, MD, author of *The Mindful Twenty-Something: Life Skills to Handle Stress . . . and Everything Else.* Dr. Rogers is a psychiatrist for Duke University's Counseling and Psychological Services and developed

Koru, a mindfulness program for young adults.

"We get in the habit of being pretty judgmental or critical of ourselves and our human foibles, and it becomes a reflex to be judgmental and critical of others, too," Dr. Rogers said.

"My students are always talking about how, when they started looking at the way their mind works and what their thoughts are, how much of it is criticisms of themselves."

The way this stops, Dr. Rogers said, is through mindfulness—sitting quietly, and observing your thoughts without judgment or criticism. Mindfulness, really, is just listening to your own brain. Then you do it again and again and again and again, until your brain quiets down a little bit and you start being able to let the negative thoughts pass you by rather than getting stuck in a spiral.

"If you're willing to practice bringing your attention to the present, letting go of those judgments and criticisms, you don't have to force yourself to be nonjudgmental," Dr. Rogers said. "It just kind of happens."

Plus, she said, mindfulness brings peace of mind.

"If you want to have a happy, grounded life, your behaviors have to be in concert with your values, and in order to do that, you have to know what your values are," Dr. Rogers said. "Mindfulness allows you the wisdom to see what you *do* care about, and it also gives you the discernment to see when you're not putting your energies in the right directions."

When you find yourself ABSOLUTELY NEEDING RIGHT NOW to correct something about yourself (or others), take that pause. What about this bothers me? *Why* is this a problem? Am I feeling unnecessary guilt and shame? Before you act on it, take a step back from your own thought process for a moment and examine it. Prod at it. See if it's real and where it might be coming from. Is this truly a situation as urgent and dire as it initially seemed, or like so much mental flotsam, does it evaporate when

Wait, stop! I hear you! I know we *all* know that mindfulness is important, in the same way that we know that eating dark greens and changing your car's oil are important. But please, please try, because those mental muscles are absolutely key to graciousness.

exposed to the sunlight of your rational mind?

But be forewarned: As discussed throughout this chapter, the inside of your skull can be a pretty unfriendly place. Though you should absolutely start today (please?), there are smaller steps you can take that maybe will pay dividends more quickly.

Here, I am thrilled to introduce Brian McCook, better known to the world as Katya Zamolodchikova, who is the most lovely and kind and thoughtful and hilarious drag queen that this world has yet produced, though Brian, being a very modest person, would deny this.

He, like me (and many, many others of us out there), is a person who has a LOT of anxiety, self-doubt, and depression. But he has some excellent strategies to keep those particular demons settled down.

"I treat myself like a sensitive friend—that fragile, emotional, and yes, perhaps sometimes disturbed best friend you've had. Maybe she's been through a lot! Maybe she *continues* to go through a lot, but you really, really like her," Brian said. "And you know things are hard, but the key is that there is the very real promise of development, improvement, getting better."

What does that look like, I asked, in real life?

"If it's not helpful, I don't say it, or at least I don't focus on it," Brian said. "I try to have this disciplined attitude of, 'NO, Brenda, NO. If you're NOT going to learn from this, then move on. Or if you are going to learn from it, good, do that, then *move on.*"

In fact, Brian actually named his mean, internal monologue 'Brenda,' as in "Okay, Brenda. Thanks, Brenda. Heard you the first time, Brenda."

Plus—and this is another arena in which thinking of others is best practiced—chances are that unless you are practicing meditation and/or mindfulness or are a super-advanced human who composts things and loves yourself, time spent in your own head is a bad plan. The State Department has issued a travel advisory for it: You're not *banned* from going there, per se, but you should definitely keep your wits about you and pay attention to what's happening and not spend hours wandering aimlessly around a dangerous mental neighborhood.

Past Regrets Workspace Fun Time!

1. Take a deep breath, then write down *every single thing you've ever done that you regret* in the space below.

   _____

   _____

   (Add additional libraries of regret if need be.)

2. What can you do to change how these things happened? 🍍

   _____

   _____

3. What is something good you can do *right this minute*?

   _____

   _____

4. Cool. Go do that because that is something that positively changes the world. Please draw a picture of yourself sleeping snuggly on the belly of a giant, loving otter below:

🍍 The correct answer is "nothing," though any synonym is acceptable that conveys your complete inability to change the past.

He paused.

"And no more dwelling. I do it all the time, or I used to, and it's almost this delusional thing where you're trying to rewrite the past. Are you a magician?"

Oh, the enchanted and enchanting world of Dwelling on the Past! How often I find myself lured by its groan-y siren song! Dwelling's voice, incidentally, is a *perfect* synthesis of that one coworker you just cannot ever like and a Kardashian making an "Eeeehhhhhhhhhhhhhh!" noise.

But what do we accomplish by dwelling? It's not as if beating ourselves up for long enough or feeling sufficiently guilty will grant us the power to change the past! Yet we think and think and think mean little peanut thoughts🍍 about This One Thing (but also those 1,845 Other Things), as if there will be a moment, when we have dwelled hard enough and sadly enough, that eventually a new wind blows us clean, whistles through us like we are the most delicate lace, tumbles the offending incident down the street, never to be heard from or thought about again.

We act as though whatever we did will be undone with enough self-criticism, that we can rewind the tape and just tape right over that (mistake, relationship, fateful moment, awful reality that might be incredibly perfect if only we had made a different decision 12 years ago) by just hating ourselves enough. Does that sound

---

🍍 My mother often describes someone as acting or looking like a mean little peanut. A True-Life Example:

As Kelly walks through the big revolving door at the airport, she expects her mother, Barbara, will join her since those compartments are like 25 feet in diameter. But Barbara, in *very cautious* Barbesque fashion, will wait 25 seconds for the other compartment to come around, because safety first, and also one time she saw a kid get his foot stuck in an escalator.

By this point, Kelly is outside the door and, to teach her mother a lesson, hits the disabled button. The revolving door, which had been at about 1.5 rpm, now slows down to 0.5 rpm. For 45 glorious seconds, Kelly watches in delight as her mother is trapped in a giant revolving door, but hey, at least she is safe!

Even before Barbara emerges from her slow, safe prison, Kelly can hear her mother's incensed voice. "Oh my GOD, I cannot BELIEVE you, what the FRICK is wrong with you? KELLY! STOP MAKING THAT MEAN PEANUT FACE! Oh my golly gumpo," which is something Barbara often says, to the delight of her daughters.

familiar? Does that sound productive? Right.

I asked Brian how he stops dwelling.

"It's almost like running away," he said, and here I will note that in some cases, like bears or exes who send you a bunch of sad Facebook messages late at night, running away from self-abusive thoughts is *precisely what one should do*. But it feels weird, Brian said.

"Perhaps because I'm such a notorious dweller, it feels like I'm not dealing with something I need to," he said. "But the reality is, like, I am just holding on to a dead squirrel. Bury the squirrel. Just put down that dirty plate."

> "We venture to express a hope that they will *get rid of the present slavish uniformity*—that what is becoming to each may be worn without fear of unfashionableness, and that in this way we may see every woman dressed somewhat differently and to her own best advantage, and the *proportion of beauty largely increased*, as it would, thereby, most assuredly be."

–The *PMRE*, on slaying, sartorially speaking

These dead squirrels are what trap you in the past, taking your attention away from the present, which, if you'll remember, is the only time in which we can do anything.

Don't get me wrong: You can do this in a way that is gentle and does not lead you to berate yourself for berating yourself. Absolutely be *so polite and gentle* to yourself! Just say, "Gosh, Brain of Mine, thank you so much for that thought about whether me and him could've worked if 43 things had happened differently and also if I was a different person. You know, I'm actually trying *really hard* to focus on this presentation for work right now. So let's just table that thought, and if it's *really, really* important, we can talk about it later."

You can do this again and again, all day, always, because those critical judgments—of yourself, of others, of how things right now are not *exactly* how you want them to be—are not particularly useful. Just like with your mindfulness practice, you can train yourself

A FUN, DAY-LONG EXPERIMENT
that will leave you Startled!

Here's how it goes, tiny gems:

1. Get a little bitty spiral-bound notebook.

2. Label said notebook Mean Peanut Thoughts.

3. Set it by your bed the night before.

4. *Every single time you say or feel something negative about yourself*—in the morning, through the day, into the evening, and right before you go to bed—just go ahead and put a little tally mark.

5. How many tally marks is that?

6. How helpful were those thoughts to your life?

7. Rip that sheet out.

8. Cross out *Mean* on the cover and write *Sweet*.

9. Use the rest of your Sweet Peanut Thoughts notebook to write kind li'l notes to people you love (maybe only two sentences!).

to move beyond those thoughts rather than get stuck in them.

In *Everyday Zen*, Joko Beck describes two kinds of thoughts.

"There is nothing wrong with thinking in the sense of what I call 'technical thinking.' We have to think in order to walk from here to the corner, to bake a cake, or to solve a physics problem.

Joko Beck is amazing and she was my Grannybarb's guru and now that Grannybarb is no longer relaxing on this terrestrial plane, I have all her books. When she liked something, GB would put a delicate pencil line in the margin, stretching down through the words that moved her. If something was REALLY stupendous, she might add a tiny ! beside it.

That use of the mind is fine . . . but opinions, judgments, memories, dreaming about the future—90 percent of the thoughts in our head have no essential reality."

Plus, she said, only one of those two kinds of thinking ever gets anything done.

"No matter what the work is, it should be done with effort and total attention to what's in front of our nose," she writes. "If we are cleaning the oven, we should just totally do that and also be aware of any thoughts that interrupt the work."

My internal monologue while cleaning the oven goes something like this: "Oh my God, this is DISGUSTING, is this a STALAG-MITE made of BURNED GOUDA? How did this *happen*? Why is the oven so foul, and why do *I* have to clean it? Could I trick someone else into cleaning it? Why clean it, anyway? Perhaps by throwing off the *shackles* that *bind me* to this *godforsaken kitchen appliance,* I could Lean In to Not Cleaning the Oven, and perhaps, while I'm at it, do my small part to crush the Patriarchy!"

No, Joko says. Not this way. *Just clean the oven.*

If you, like me, find this very, very hard, you can take another tip from Joko and practice labeling your thoughts as a way of understanding what your internal monologue actually consists of.

"I am having a thought about the past. I am having a thought about being angry. I am having a thought about myself. I am having a thought about how something is not exactly as I want it to be. I am having a thought about being angry. I am having a thought about myself."

This, Joko says, eventually helps you realize how boringly repetitive those mean peanut thoughts are.

"After all," she writes, "who wants to watch the same movie 500 times?"

Lizzie Post, who is the great-grandaughter of Emily Post and was my celebrity friendship crush except that now we're *actually friends* (!!!! :) <3), said that when she is hurting or in doubt, she likes to take a moment to examine the story she is telling herself.

"Let's say—and this is more personal—but let's say that I'm

(continued on page 112)

Theories of Grace

Dorothy Buckhanan Wilson is the international president of Alpha Kappa Alpha Sorority, Inc. She is also, objectively, a lioness, and even her walk conveys both authority and warmth. When I met her, she was just wrapping up a very successful convention and had turned her sights to the upcoming international convention, which would draw somewhere around 30,000 women to Atlanta. She's a longtime corporate executive, most recently as senior vice president of Goodwill Industries, where she oversaw a $25 million budget in Wisconsin and Chicago. She's also established two endowed scholarships, has an honorary doctorate of letters, and . . . you know what? Honestly, someone should write a book about her, and if I was going to accurately reflect everything that she's achieved, it would take that amount of space. Basically, if you can imagine an impressive thing, chances are very good she's done it.

I think the art of grace, for me, comes not in doing those things that come naturally but in those situations where you find yourself tested and stressed and conflicted and you're still doing the right thing and still exhibiting grace.

To me, service [to others] is the rent you pay for living on earth, and you have a fundamental obligation to give back, especially those of us who have been afforded the opportunity to be in a situation where we can advocate for ourselves and advocate for others.

I was the first person in my family, out of 33 cousins, to attend and graduate from college. Mind you, some of those same cousins have since gone back to school and gotten advanced degrees.

I went and got a master's degree

at a time when a lot of women weren't going to get their master's . . . I was a younger woman in a classroom full of men, and half of them felt like I didn't deserve my spot. But I knew something they didn't know—when it came to working and being resilient and having a compass—this is where I'm going, and I'm going to get there. I knew what was inside of me.

My motto has always been: Make a difference to those around you by changing the game. Don't be content doing what has always been done. Think of how you can make it better, how you can make it more efficient, how you can leave it better than it was when you found it. Everything that I do, even in my personal life, I think, How do I leave this better than when I found it? Is there any tangible evidence of me having been here? What can I point to that I can say I changed the results of the situation?

At the end of the day, I understand that there are certain situations I'd never be in and certain breaks I'd never get simply because of my skin color and the fact that I am a woman. With that being said, I've truly optimized every opportunity that has come my way. I always made sure I was prepared.

If you are gracious and kind and polite, people will help you. If you are rude and obnoxious and overbearing, why would anyone want to help you do anything? You can catch a lot more flies with honey than vinegar. You can be true to who you are.

I always dress nice because I don't want there to be any confusion on who is in charge when I walk in the building.

doubting my worth or my lovability or my desirability to men because I'm a single gal and I'm looking for a lifelong partner and I haven't found him," she said. "And then I might start to think, 'Maybe I'll never find someone, maybe I have bad timing, maybe I'll always be alone.'

"What I do is try to bring myself back to truth. Doubt is worries and fears, and worries and fears aren't always real. So what's the real story of my life?

"I've had wonderful relationships over the years that did not end in marriage or partnership because I chose that. You start counteracting the fears with as much truth as you can find while still being a humble and reasonable human being. I try to focus on what I *know* to be true and move forward from that point."

There is one kind of thought that's always useful and always gracious. That kind of thought is, "What can I do for someone else?"

This kind of thought makes the world, and you, a better place. This kind of thought jolts you out of self-loathing or self-congratulating and makes you bigger. *This is the actual magic.* This is the balm that soothes that itchy soul rash.

The only caveat here is to remember that your needs (needs, not fears) are real; they are neither more nor less important than everyone else's needs and they deserve to be listened to.

The dear friend filter also works here. If your friend had a fever of 102°F, would you recommend she still go through with that dinner party she's hosting? If your friend had a boss that expected 70 hours of work per week but paid her for 40, would you encourage her to stand up for herself in a respectful way that also acknowledges her talents, her dedication, and her worth? If your wonderful friend was hurting herself by making the same mistake again and again, would you write her off as a helpless, pitiable idiot or would you try to help her figure out a better path?

Viewing and treating yourself as a person worthy of dignity and respect makes it easier to be your highest self. It will allow you to stand up for yourself in ways that don't unnecessarily hurt others.

It will allow you to go to bed at night knowing that you've acted and communicated in accordance with your values. It gives you the ability to step away from yourself for a moment, to know that while yes, you feel sad right now, that's okay. You won't feel sad forever and in fact can feel a lot of other positive things simultaneously with your sadness.

When you meet someone who knows *exactly* who they are and what they're about, it is so lovely. They are so anchored not to things or situations or people but to their own serenity.

When you *are* that person—and it's not impossible, it just takes work every day, every hour, every minute—then you are the one who moves through the ocean like a grand steamship. You move steadily, storms do not rock you, you're always on course, and you have four smokestacks and a *bunch* of awesome teak deck chairs. So noble! A triumph of man. You. *You* are the triumph.

Well-known but little-absorbed fact: You won't feel *any feeling* forever. They feel permanent, but they aren't. Unless the feeling in question is fear that when you open the hood of your running car an angry opossum will jump out at you because that *did* happen to me one time and it touched my hair and I *always do not want that to happen again.*

Oh my gosh, I love steamships, I really do.

CHAPTER FIVE

Gracious IN, AROUND & GENERALLY REGARDING THE Home

One time, after relaying to my mother how impressed I was by my then-boyfriend's apartment,🍍 she nodded matter-of-factly.

"Well," she said, "the Dutch are very house-proud."

This delighted me. One, I believe it is okay to make sweeping, benign generalizations about northern European countries.🍍🍍

Two, it was the first time I'd ever heard that wonderful phrase "house-proud"—so simple! Two syllables packed with nuance! I love it and use it all the time.

I can't speak to my mother's statement on personal habitat pride as a trademark of the Dutch, but I suppose it seems right. A people who had a historically important tulip mania probably still have a culture of keeping things neat.

I'm someone who has not, historically, been particularly house-proud. House-anxious, house-despairing, house-shamed, house–HOW DID ALL THESE FRUIT FLIES GET IN HERE; GOOD GOD THERE ARE THOUSANDS OF THEM; NOW A BUNCH ARE IN MY MOUTH BECAUSE I WAS YELLING!, yes. House-proud, not so much.

But now I am. I *love* walking into my house every time, because

---

🍍 Seriously! He was 22 and had things like antique wall sconces.

🍍🍍 Ben was only half Dutch, which to me implies an *extreme* dominance of this house pride gene, if it exists, which obviously it doesn't.

it's mine and because I've learned a lot of valuable lessons in my ongoing cold war with fruit flies. 🍍

Of course, the first half of that statement is what makes my house important to me and worth caring for and making into a place that I both love and like.

Remember how in every chapter I've hammered on the fact that we can't do anything to change other people's behavior? Or life happenings, generally? And all we can do is the right action within our power?

Well, your house is *yours*, and you get to control this little space (perhaps the only space in the world under your purview!) and shape it and make it into what you want. And even if you don't like it right now, you probably love it for the following reasons:

1. It keeps you warm and dry when you sleep!

2. It contains almost everything you own and love!

3. People whom you don't care for are *not allowed* to come inside! Usually!

4. It is the only place you can waft about naked or cry/rage/scream/throw a glass for dramatic effect, say the filthiest things, AND watch every single episode of *My Big Fat American Gypsy Wedding* without being judged. 🍍🍍

Graciousness at home is the exact same thing as graciousness anywhere else—simple but not easy, something that you can always practice again and again. Dedicate yourself to whatever is in front of you, whether that's a guest or a pile of clean laundry. And yes, you can certainly do the bare minimum for both of those, but I

🍍 Namely, don't leave ripe fruit out. That's actually the only lesson I've learned, but on the upside, apparently it's only one anyone who struggles with these devil-flecks needs to learn. My friend Kim noted that it's also important not to leave a bunch of ketchup in your garbage can, but *why was it there in the first place, Kim?* What were you *doing*?

🍍🍍 COME ON, THOSE DRESSES! I am not ashamed to live my best life, and my best life for sure includes that show.

would always recommend taking a little bit of extra time to do it well. You have to fold those clothes anyway—why not take a few more seconds per garment and lovingly fold them in a tidy, satisfying way?

When you are present and mindful in an environment filled with things you don't resent, you *see* it. You pay attention to it, and this attention leads to the ability to stave off chaos with minimal fuss. If this is not something you've made a regular habit of, you may be surprised at what you see when you look around you: Were you aware of that little nest of single socks eagerly mingling on the floor of your closet? When was the last time you took a moment to admire the beautiful wall hanging/sculpture/knickknack from your favorite vacation?

I hope that you, dear reader, absolutely *adore* your habitat. In fact, if your home is in perfect order, if you have mastered the fine craft of hosting, if you know exactly how to *be* a fabulous guest, then please feel free to skip merrily ahead in this book, or tend to the hydrangeas that bloom in your yard like so many heavenly spheres, or . . . I don't know, whatever your heart calls you toward.

However, *I* must write this chapter because *my* home, much as I adore it, has a long, long way to go.

Messy Lady Confession Time!

Y'all, I am not a gifted housekeeper. It has never, ever come naturally to me. I was always the kid with the room that was essentially an avalanche of books and art supplies with half-eaten candy and

> "It is not pleasant to be a guest in a house where you perceive that your hostess is continually and fretfully on the watch, lest some almost imperceptible injury should accrue to the furniture."

—Miss Leslie, on why you should buy furniture meant for humans to use and not, say, a severely modern white couch that spontaneously self-generates a stain whenever gazed upon by human eyes

wrappers peppered throughout. To this day, I have to remind myself that bowls with leftover kimchi in them should not just be left under your bed, *even for a night or two.*

Dishes stack up, and tumbleweeds of Eleanor hair, made up of loooooong wavy white dog fur (seriously, it looks like it was crimped and each strand is somehow 8 inches long) tumble cheerfully from place to place, sometimes stacking softly on one another to create great spheres as much as a foot across. Sometimes, on my side of the bed, clothes that I have worn pile up like a soft haystack, which then collapses to become a soft ground cover. Just yesterday, I was rooting around in the hamper🍍 and heard crinkling. What should I find but a tiny, unopened bag of crunchy Cheetos! This was dubbed the Brown Family Miracle of September 2016.

But I have learned to be reasonably tidy, because otherwise, instead of tackling the problem, it is so easy to let everything pile up, just feeling defeated and avoiding having people over (in the case of unexpected visitors, you scramble and put everything in any drawer).

My strategy for this is simple. I need to have definitive answers for the following for *every object in my house*:

1. Do I love this? (And yes, I love my can opener for, though humble, it *always opens whatever can I want it to!*)

2. Why do I let this remain in my personal space? *Love is not always enough.*

3. Where does this item live?

Then, because I am an animist and pretty sure that everything I own has a soul, I feel a little bit on the hook as the legal guardian of these items. Oh, no! This nail polish has become separated from his relatives! Let me return him to them so they stop worrying. Then, nail polish goes in nail polish box. Repeat endlessly for every

🍍 DEFINITELY NOT for a pair of leggings I wanted to wear. I would *never* do such a thing, and frankly I'm a little insulted that you implied it.

Adjectives That Do and Do Not Apply to a Gracious Home

YES!
- Welcoming
- Cared for
- Tidy
- Comfortable
- Lived in
- Full of interesting things

NO!
- Spotless
- Minimalist
- Sterile
- Intimidating
- Hoardery
- Sticky
- Oppressively Pinterest-y

item. I don't like being away from home; I like feeling in place, and gosh darn it, it's the least I can do for them, that little bit of comfort and belonging.

I talked to Beverly Gianna—a *full-time* volunteer as an ombudsman for a public hospital—about how she manages to stay on top of all of the hundreds of e-mails, calls, and texts she gets from work

Beverly Gianna is *such* a treasure of a woman, and I had grown up hearing a bajillion stories about her from my mom when, back in the early '80s, they worked together on the New Orleans World's Fair PR. In fact, Beverly had been regularly used as an example of How to Be in our home, because Beverly kicked everyone's ass in PR *and* she is beyond funny and charming.

I didn't meet Beverly in person until I was writing this book, but it took not even 30 seconds to see why, decades later, my mom still talks about her. She apologized to me ahead of time that her phones would beep sometimes and she would need to check them, because as the ombudsman, she takes calls from distressed family members who are worried that their loved one isn't getting the right care, and Beverly is in charge of investigating and helping.

She's one of those people who retired, then promptly unretired, and also the front room of her house is all glass and what little wall is there is painted yellow and there are plants inside and outside, and as soon as I saw it, I *literally* shivered with delight and whispered to myself, "Ah! Such a solarium!" She did not hear me, thank God.

while still maintaining a semblance of her own life and sanity.

"Well, I don't know! But I guess it's like housework," she said. "Someone asked me once how I keep my house so tidy, and I guess it's because I do things as they need to be done. I don't lay a piece of clothing down, I hang it up. I don't stack a lot of papers; I open them, discard the envelopes, and put them in piles, then put the piles away. I clean my shoes before I put them on the shelf."

About your stuff...

I do not know your heart or your mind, dear reader. I don't know what your most beautiful moment in this life is; I don't know the things that wake you up from a dead sleep in terror.

But I do know one thing: You have too much stuff.

Well, you *almost certainly* have too much stuff, because almost everyone has too much stuff. We don't mean to, yet we live in a capitalist society, so we acquire things because we needed them or we wanted them or they are pretty or were too good of a deal to pass up or we inherited them or someone brought this item into our life and for difficult-to-articulate reasons, we can't let it go.

There was a book that you may have heard of, since every single person in the world read it: Marie Kondo's *The Life-Changing Magic of Tidying Up*. I avoided this book like the plague for years, because I assumed it would make pack-ratty me feel the worst about everything.

No, no. It was delightful, and SO WONDERFUL to pare down my belongings.

I won't summarize the book, but basically, if you do not *love a thing* or at least *love it because you need it*, it should not be in your house. Unlovable (to you) things may live any number of places in this world, but they shouldn't live with you.

Thank them for their service, then donate, recycle, or discard them.

Just across Lake Pontchartrain, in my hometown of Covington, Louisiana, Virginia Provosty (do you remember her from Chapter 1?) oversees what I consider to be a nearly perfect house, made more so because it feels like it just *is* comfortable, interesting, and clean, and not that Virginia is running around right before company gets there.

"I do run around and pick things up. I order the environment, but it can't be overly ordered—simplicity is truly the answer here," Virginia said. "The house itself is what's supposed to be embracing—it's warm, it's comfortable. I sit down when my company comes, and I'm *with* them. It took me years to learn that! The world is a frenetic place; let your home be someone's comfort zone.

"I remember when you and (my son) Townsend were itty-bitty, my father drove to my house, and you two were crawling around, and I remember saying, 'I have to sweep the floor,' and my father said, 'You can do that when I'm gone.' And now? Now that he's gone, gone, *gone*? Do I *ever* regret spending 1 minute with my back to him?"

I'm going to launch into some tips from the gracious here, but before I do, a gentle reminder that while these principles are wonderful and can go a long way toward creating a comfy, welcoming place, the most important thing is a house that makes *you* happy. As my friend Carol Kaplan would say, people should match their homes. It's not that the things in your house need to match each other, but they should match you.

Nora—do you remember darling Nora? Who is like an angel AND a fairy AND a giant smile? Well, she's back in this chapter, and *her mother, Mary Jane Murrell, is here, too!* Interviewing both of them was beyond adorable, because both of them were *constantly* saying that I should really be interviewing the other one. #motherdaughtergoals!

When I asked Nora how her home is so beautiful, she said, "Oh my GOSH, you are SO KIND! Well, you know, I just think about where a person's eyes would go—when they walk in the door, what will they see? If they're going into the living room, what would their eyes land on? And then I take that little spot and make sure there is something beautiful there for them."

So, let us, for a moment, be a guest in your own home. Walk up to the door, and open it. What greets you? Where do your eyes go?

I don't care if you have one of those New York apartments where the first thing you see is the backside of the toilet—*make that the most beautiful toilet backside you can.*

Mary Jane agreed with this and said that no matter how messy the house generally is, she tries to keep the front room neat so that if someone stops by, there is somewhere that's comfortable.

"I think a gracious home is a fresh, clean, cared-for, but also comfortable home where you can sit down anywhere without feeling like you're messing things up," Mary Jane said. "Maybe it's not picture-perfect but it's really comfortable. There're fresh flowers stuck in a vase—nothing stiff or fussy."

She—and everyone I talked to for this chapter—mentioned having flowers around. I puzzled about this at first before I realized that flowers achieve three excellent goals:

1. They're fresh and natural and smell nice.

2. They are totally optional and universally beloved, which means

3. They are quite gracious things to have around.

"Flowers are so important," Virginia said. "Plant them in your garden and bring them inside, but don't neglect the ditch weeds. If I'm on a walk, and there in the ditch, I see cattails or wildflowers, I'll grab them. If it's beautiful, if God put it in front of you, then you were meant to see and enjoy it."

I know that floral arrangements are not free and available to everyone. But if you have a yard, if you go on walks, or basically if you have any exposure to greenery that is not a place where it's totally inappropriate to take little cuttings—then *do it.*

During the winter, I'll go outside and cut some Douglas fir branches, holly and red berries. In the spring and summer, there're

In defense of beauty...

Beauty, for us women, is such a loaded word, right? There's the superficiality so often applied to it, that in humans, it's skin-deep (true!), that to love or pursue beautiful things implies materialism, frivolity, and not caring about what is *really important.*

It's as though loving a beautiful vintage couch takes up all the space in your brain that would otherwise be dedicated to struggling for justice, that if you were not buying this throw pillow, you'd be spending that time and money building wells in sub-Saharan Africa. Which, obviously, is a *great* thing to do, and very gracious. If you find that simply *thinking* about what you like to look at every day saps you of any shred of humanity or compassion, then, yeah, I guess, definitely examine your priorities.

For the rest of us . . . we would never argue against, say, food that is delicious or music that is wonderful to listen to. No one would argue that to be a good feminist, one must eschew anything that smells nice in lieu of the most pragmatic odor. Why must taking and creating visual pleasure in our surroundings be labeled as something shameful?

The world is absolutely *full* of ugly things that we must see. In fact, to *always* turn away from that ugliness, whether it be environmental degradation or images of war, *isn't* very gracious, because it implies that you would rather be comfortable than be present to your fellow humans.

But because of this, it is a good and proper thing to create that beauty where you can. Bring lovely order out of chaos. Celebrate whatever it is that, when you gaze upon it, makes you smile.

The most pragmatic and therefore democratic odor being, of course, canola oil. Also, did you know that canola was originally known as rapeseed oil? Kudos on a much-needed rebrand.

dandelions in a field, if nothing else. If it's your style, get a few sweet little bud vases that can be grouped together with a single blossom in each.

Hot Tip: Mix in lots of greenery with your flowers—tree branches with small leaves, fern leaves, what*ever.* This plumps things up, looks beautiful, and as a bonus, leaves your flower reserves larger.

The other thing that I always, *always* noticed: When I came in, I *immediately* wanted to sit down. This can be chalked up, in part, to my hatred of standing/walking and a desire always to be as close to lying down as soon as possible—but there's nothing like walking into a home with a nice comfy something inviting you to take a load off after your journey is over.

What's more, all the seating was *comfortable.* Not like La-Z-Boy comfortable, but squishy cushions, soft throws, a variety of seat heights. One of my favorite spaces that most embodied these principles was what I described as the solarium of Beverly Gianna. The room is painted yellow, is flooded with light, and has garden views from the big windows. Inside, the furniture was rattan with *huge* cushions, plus there were big, happy plants in pots, so it felt like we were both inside and outside.

"I love beautiful, luxurious fabrics that are more natural and washable like linens—they can create a neutral sort of background for everything, and they're just comfortable and casual looking but also beautiful," Mary Jane said. "And that's the great thing—it is washable, so if someone spills, I just pick it up and wash it and it's as good as new. The linen gets a little more rumply and worn-looking and gets the prettiest patina on it."

So, when you are contemplating that furniture acquisition, ask yourself: Is this comfortable? Will it look better with age, or would the slightest hint of red wine ruin it? Is it neutral enough to play well with whatever little details or big centerpieces I want to put behind it?

Mary Jane takes inspiration from places she travels to rather than hewing to whatever is trendiest. If she goes somewhere and *loves* the color schemes or the lines or whatever it may be, she examines how to bring those influences into her house.

She said that for several decades, she absolutely *loved* Mexican folk art and filled her home with those bright colors. Now, she said, she tends to favor French decor, which is a little bit more subtle in its colors. Luckily, her furniture is versatile enough to match both.

"The trends of decorating sort of come and go, but the main thing, I think, is how to place furniture and create a conversation area that will stay the same, and change the small things every so often," she said.

> "Your first object should be to make your guests feel at home. This they never can do while your needless bustle and obtrusive attentions constantly remind them that they are not at home, and perhaps make them wish they were."
>
> —Preach, the *PMRE*

She and Nora have an incredible strategy for refreshing or resuscitating hard furniture like chairs, tables, armoires, dressers, and anything else made of a hard material: chalk paint!

"It's the neatest kind of paint," Mary Jane said, as I adored her even more for deciding that one style of paint can definitively be called "the neatest."

"You don't need to do any kind of sanding or priming before you paint, it will stick to anything, and it comes in super-beautiful colors. You can go get an inexpensive thing from Goodwill and paint it, and it just looks like a million dollars."

I cannot personally attest to the power of chalk paint because I am *all about the spray paint*, in the same way that Anna Wintour is *all about fashion and terror*. If a surgeon were to crack open my ribs and delicately incise my heart, there would probably be a ventricle solely dedicated to my love of spray painting.

A significant other once had to have a spray paintervention with me, in which he calmly but assertively noted that I was now on round two or three of spray-painting the same objects, and he was glad I was happy, but could I please, *please* agree to a temporary moratorium on spray-painting furniture in Easter egg colors?

But I cannot help it, and here's why. If I had 80 million dollars and could shop solely at beautiful, high-end furniture stores, duh, obviously that's exactly what I would do. I would order *precisely* what was the most beautiful in *exactly* the wood tone or hue that it would look best in. But I don't and I can't. I do have Craigslist and Goodwill and *spray paint!*

The art of spray-painting furniture, which is *ridiculously* easy, means that *any piece of wood furniture can be any color you want it to be!* You can grab that amazing dresser that is, unfortunately, a wood tone best described as "old bruise at twilight." All you have to look for is quality and whether the lines and style of the piece match your home and aesthetic.

That ugly dark brown frame could be a cheerful gold frame! That scratched-up headboard could be a sunny, buttery yellow! I could keep listing items and colors here, but you get the idea!

A gracious home tells the story of the person who lives in it—not in the "HEY, LOOK AT ALL THE TIMES I'VE BEEN ON A MAGAZINE COVER!" way but rather in a way that invites the gaze and then conversation.

Here is a True Spray-Paint Story. I had these beautiful fawn-colored boots that I would have never been able to afford but they were on 85 percent clearance. We had three beautiful weeks together, those boots and me, until the Beef Fat Incident, which I still am not totally okay with, but suffice it to say that I got second *and* third opinions from leather cleaners in town, all of whom said that my boots would never be okay and I should throw them in the garbage.

What these leather cleaners *didn't* take into account was the powerful, symbiotic relationship I have with spray paint! If I was going to throw them out, I reasoned, I may as well try, right?

Since then, those boots, which "The Man" and/or Patriarchy would have had me leave for dead, have been light blue, a silvery gray, and, for the majority of the time, shiny gold. Every time I wear them, people stop me and ask where I got those gold boots. I smile, inhale, and prepare my body and soul to spread the Gospel of Spray Paint.

If you, too, wish to reach this level with me, then I'd recommend covering all areas of the boot you don't want gold with masking tape, and just giving them a light, quick spray every month or so as needed.

TLC/HGTV/Crime+Investigation executives, if you are reading this, I am *so open* to developing as a reality series. Starring me. Where I solve people's problems by giving them advice, then spray painting. Like, *Spray Chronicles* or *The Spray Lady* or *Help! I Need Something Spray-Painted and A Stranger to Weigh In on My Life!*

Heavier is nearly always better; it should not shift or groan when you give it a firm shake, etc.

SO YOU'RE A LITTLE S.P.-CURIOUS ...

When you want to spray-paint, clean off the item first, paying special attention to any sticky spots. Mary Jane said you don't need to sand, and I've never busted out a sander, but I find using a fine sanding paper, going gently over all surfaces, tends to lead to a better result. Again, wipe away the sanding mess you've made, making sure everything is quite dry, and you're ready!

For nearly all paints—heck, this includes nail polish!—you want very even, very light coats with plenty of time to dry in between. For spray paint, I'd highly recommend getting the little spray paint gun that will allow you to hold down the nozzle without giving yourself permanent hand cramps. Beyond this, dear ones, I'll let you take to the Internet, which has enough furniture-painting tutorials that you could read nothing but, until you die. But don't do that. Life is for living . . . and also for spray painting.

If you're me.

In my living room, things on the wall don't match perfectly, but all of them have a story. There are a few big photo prints from a story I did on Miss Rodeo Oregon's year in the run-up to the Miss Rodeo America pageant. There's a block print a friend did of my precious Grannybarb sipping out of an airplane Bacardi bottle at Christmas. There's the *Matrangela*—a ceramic angel with enormous hips holding an armful of fruit, a traditional Sicilian gift for a bride-to-be that my in-laws brought me from their travels.

These things, when I look at them, bring me joy. They remind me of places and people I've loved; they remind me who I am. They

That is a story for another time, but *such a story!* Rodeo queens, man! They are *something*, and I love them with all my heart.

These bottles, at least one of which was always in her fanny pack, sometimes contained booze but more often water. Taking little sips relieved her throat, she said, and she enjoyed seeing other people's reactions to her taking a swig while in line at the grocery store.

Decoration vs. Clutter

Oh, how I *wish* I could have every single thing I own (with the possible exception of my more world-weary, jaded underwear) in view!

A little hissy voice in my brain whispers, "Yes, this window ledge looks *okay* right now, but wouldn't it look *better* if you just went ahead and put a bunch of random stuff on it? Maybe some of those plastic wind-up toys from your childhood? And the Mexican wrestler finger puppet that you got in your stocking in Christmas 2007? Maybe tape some ribbon on there, because we're all going to die someday? Yesssss, perfect, that's a love. Oh, they've fallen! Well, pick them back up! Again and again! As you will do *literally every day!*"

I cannot explain this compulsion. I *can*, however, offer these wise words from Mary Jane, which were shared with her by her dear friend Harry:

There should be a 12-inch rule. Nothing smaller than 12 inches in the house, as far as accessories go, because it makes things look like clutter if there are too many small things.

But take heart! This does not mean you need to use a ruler as your scythe, sacrificing all small things to the god of Good Taste.

"Smaller items are really cute grouped together," Mary Jane said. "If you get a little collection of small things and group them, that can make a big statement."

Truth. But for those of you who share my inclination to add and add and add until the windowsill is too full for anyone to ever reach over and open the window, remember that restraint is a virtue.

also tell my guests something about me, create an opportunity for starting a conversation, and set a tone for what kind of home a traveler has just meandered into.

When I walk into a home with beautiful *and* interesting things to look at, it's wonderful. I can ask who earned this medal from the City of New Orleans and how? I can ask about this picture of a beautiful woman in the 1940s posing near an enormous plane propeller—

who is she? What is she doing next to that propeller?

All of that is to say: Don't buy decorative items that are produced en masse because they are pretty and cheaply available at IKEA (unless you really need them or absolutely love them!). Think about building your home decor as a lifelong project. Buy a print or piece of art every time you travel that will remind you of that place. Blow up your favorite photo of the view from a hike you took, even if that picture isn't magical to anyone but you. Figure out how to display those special things that have accumulated in your life so that you see them often and get a chance to tell, or just remember, their stories.

Also, remember that not everything has to be out all the time. Carol Kaplan mentioned that she likes to swap things in and out to keep it interesting, and sometimes she'll go through the house and box up everything that she feels has been in the spotlight too long and replace them from a box of items similarly gathered 6 months or a year ago.

Lighting

You know, biologically speaking, if it weren't for light, we wouldn't *have* vision or interior decor as we know it. Think of it! All decor would be judged solely on squishiness; we would live in a world where the beanbag chair was king! That doesn't sound so bad, and yet light *does* exist and makes an enormous difference on how everything looks.

Mary Jane said the biggest small thing you can do for your house is *dimmers*. And, in wonderful news, it is *not all that hard to change a light switch to a dimmer!* You will need about 45 minutes plus around $15 for the dimmer itself. The Internet will tell you how. If this frightens you, that's okay and probably sensible, but know that a good electrician could bang this out in a very quick time frame.

"A dimmer can create a different ambience for whatever you're going for," Mary Jane said. "They can totally transform a room . . . in the evening, when you're having dinner, dimmers make it soft and romantic so you can bring in a lot of candles."

(continued on page 132)

10 USEFUL Dining TIPS

"A young man or a young woman, unaccustomed to the settled observances of such occasions, can hardly pass through a severer ordeal than a formal dinner. Its terrors, however, are often greatly magnified."

—A Pocket Manual of Republican Etiquette (PMRE)

1. At least once—and I know this is painful—film yourself eating and talking. Yes, even if you're doing the thing where you sort of shove the unswallowed food to the side. How is all that looking from an outside perspective? Optics, y'all. *Optics.*

2. Napkins go in your lap as soon as possible. Remember they're there for you! Supporting you! Helping you achieve the goal of *not* having sauce on your face *or* your white pants. They serve all sorts of useful functions including discreet removal of inedible things from your mouth, like fish bones or gristle or, I don't know, whatever you want out of your mouth *immediately.* It goes into the napkin, then gets sort of rolled in and around. At a restaurant, feel free to ask for another napkin.

3. It's immeasurably better to start eating 20 seconds later than everyone than 5 minutes before. Different people and situations have different etiquette, but unless instructed otherwise, you should not start eating until everyone is seated, everyone is served, and the host picks up his or her fork.

4. QUICK! Touch both your index fingers to your thumbs. On your left, you will see a lowercase *b*, which stands for Bread Plate (yes, this is why the universe gave us opposable thumbs!), and on your right is a lowercase *d* for Drinks. Your bread plate is to your left, and your drinks are to your right.

5. Generally speaking, implements are arranged with forks on the left, then a plate, then knives, then spoons. Daniel Post Senning suggests remembering FO(r)KS as an acronym: Forks, O (for a plate), Knives, Spoons.

6. There may be implements on the table for every course; just start with the ones outside and work your way in. As each utensil's career comes to a close, they will leave the table on the plate or in the bowl they were used for.

7. If you're ever in doubt of what to do, just look to your host. If they are picking up that inscrutable implement, then gently scratching their hand with it, well, maybe you should, too.

8. If someone asks you a question right when you have put a bite of food in your mouth, smile slightly (*lips closed,* obviously), then make a gentle "Ehhhh, what can you do?" gesture with your hands. Do not rush through that bite, as this will just make things worse.

9. This should be abundantly clear but, unless this is a work lunch and everyone else has multiple phones on the table, you should never look at yours. Generally speaking, if you're in a social situation with humans you care about, *try not to look at your phone.* However! Everyone *does* need to look at their phone occasionally, and this is why it's a great thing to ask, "Will you excuse me?" and then head to the bathroom to check your Facebook Messenger as God intended.

10. If you're not done with a course, your utensils should rest on either side of your plate, business end at the top, in a little mountain form. Think of this as a *Restful Mountain That Is Still Hungry!* When you're done, the two utensils are set parallel to each other and pointing NW on your plate. Think of this as two parallel skis, ready to zip away! And yes, I did just make that terrible mnemonic up.

In general—and I'm sure there's a scientific reason why, but I don't know it—standard sorts of overhead light fixtures just aren't that flattering or pleasant. I always, always prefer lamps, and here is where IKEA *is* my go-to.

With lamps, you can have exactly as much light as you want, where you want it. As I said, I do get these from IKEA, but I'll also happily get old lamp bases from Goodwill or garage sales. It is really, really simple to rewire them if they don't work, and nothing delights me as much as those old-fashioned cut-crystal ones.

Mary Jane also suggested another one of her friend Harry's tricks: Buy some photographer's lens filters, which are available at camera stores and even Amazon.

"You can put them inside your lamp and it makes a rosy gold light that makes everyone look gorgeous and happy and healthy—it's so flattering," she said.

Smells & how to BEND THEM TO YOUR WILL

As I believe I have already mentioned, oh man, my feet create smells that I do not always care for! So, too, does my laundry that isn't done as often as it should be, various pet items and areas, the dishes, and sometimes the sink itself. On top of all these known enemies, there's also the shadowy specter of enigmatic smells that come from nowhere and everywhere, and good Lord, did someone *leave a bunch of clams to die in the wall*?

The first step, of course, always is to clean and/or banish these smelly items. Learn from my pain, peaches, and *never ever go on vacation without taking alllllllllll the garbage, every last bit of it, outside.*

Beyond this, a quick note! For years, I assumed that once you reach a certain level of togetherness, your house just always smells terrific. Once you have leveled up sufficiently, you stop sweating and you and all your possessions radiate a subtle white floral scent.

No! Turns out, this is not how it works. Flowers, of course, make your home smell lovely, and vigilant attentiveness to smells keep the ugly ones at bay. But the true ace up your sleeve here is *expensive candles.*

I found this out by accident one Christmas. My little sister had requested a Voluspa candle, and my dad ended up getting a little one for each of us.

That candle, y'all. It deserves its own children's book: The Little Candle That Could Make My House Smell Amazing and Give Me a New Perspective on Home Odors!

Even unlit, it gave off a beautiful but delicate fragrance that slowly and surely filled the house. It burned, Hanukkah-style, for waaaaay longer than promised. Sometimes I just light it for a few minutes but smell it for hours.

Before this, I'd been wary of scented candles, because it seemed like every time I lit one, it felt like I was living inside a giant McDonald's Baked Apple Pie sleeve. Either you *couldn't* smell it or you could *only* smell it, and if you *could* smell it, it didn't smell like whatever it claimed to, but the Uncanny Valley chemical version of, say, freshly cleaned linens.

But what I've found with fancy candles—and yes, I denounce the fact that candles aren't more democratic in their pricing—is that you get a scent that moves through your home in a very different way. It's like getting a small hint of cologne when you give someone a hug versus walking past a 13-year-old who has doused himself in BRO TO THA LIMIT CATCH YOU SOME HOT BABES NO FAT CHICKS MACHO MUSTACHE BLAST body spray.

This endorsement comes straight from my heart, as I have never, ever received a dime or any merchandise from the Voluspa candle people or from any fancy creator/supplier of scented wax. But if y'all want to give me a bunch of free candles (Laguna, Tuberosa di Notte, Mokara preferred!), you know, I would be just fine with that.

I know it seems like I am just writing this book to get free candles and a show that firmly establishes me as the Bob Ross of spray-painting items. Well, fine. Aren't we *all* trying to get free candles and be as Bob Rossian as possible?

A few last notes...

There is the smallest bit of sad news to impart, followed by all of the good news.

The sad news is that your home and garden will always be works in progress and will never attain perfection. Science has yet to develop the magic wand that will, when waved, render your home more beautiful than any magazine spread, more welcoming than a perfect bath after a hideous day, and more perfect than Beyoncé. 🍍

The good news is *also* that your home and garden will always be works in progress and will never attain perfection.

So take delight in this as a project, because unlike, say, spreadsheets, this can and will bring you tangible joy in the now. Celebrate your very own Eden in a too-often disordered and disorienting world. No matter what is happening outside the walls, your little corner of it is completely yours to tend. It is up to you to figure out how much effort you *want* to put forth into making it just as you like it, and how much time you can efficiently put into keeping it that way. But commit to that time, pumpkins, because it means having guaranteed safe space in this mad, mad world we live in.

Above all, do these things so that your home feels like a beautiful sanctuary, so that you *love* it and it feels like your silent, irreplaceable ally rather than your albatross.

But also please do it in the service of one of life's greatest pleasures, which is welcoming your favorite people into your place for the sole purpose of having a delightful, diverting time—also known as entertaining!

🍍 I've heard an anecdote about Beyoncé. When she was young, her dad had her run up hills in high heels. Beyoncé is indeed the living embodiment of running up hills in high heels, so maybe he was on to something, though I cannot in good conscience endorse that parenting practice.

CHAPTER SIX

THE *of* GRACIOUS
Host & *Hosted*

Having spent the last chapter extolling the virtues of home, it is now time to examine the delicate interplay between the host and the hosted.

When I was chatting about this chapter with my darling friend Cat,❋ she pointed out something very interesting.

"It's hard and weird to be a guest," she said, "because the taboo against entering other people's dwellings or habitats is *deep,* and so when you *are* trusted and privileged enough to be in someone's house, you want to be on your best behavior, lest those privileges be taken away."

She's right! It feels like a weird ole lizard part of our brain that *doesn't want other people in our space unless we are absolutely cool with it.* Any experience of trying to enter a large animal's den/cave/giant nest❋❋ should attest that this particular social norm predates humanity.

❋ Oh, I wish y'all could meet Cat, I really do. She is *wonderful,* has big puffy blonde curly hair, and has never said a mean thing about anyone but ignorant dudes; she possesses, as she puts it, "friendly pillow energy." This is the most apt three-word description of anyone I have ever heard. Also, Cat is my only friend who is as pale as me except she has super-blonde hair, which means that I'm always pressuring her to do *American Beauty*-style tasteful nudes but with pasta instead of rose petals.

❋❋ Yes, yes, technically, I have not done this thing. BUT I would bet you a thousand dollars that lions/bears/giant birds of prey are not cool about drop-ins, even if you are totally just there to vent and brought a bottle of Pinot Grigio.

So, as no one but me says, deuces are high and *everything's wild*[note] when it comes to having people in your home or going to other people's homes. High stakes, indeed.

However, this is a wonderful time to practice taking a situation that may be very fraught and make it look like the easiest thing in the world. Strap on those dancin' (or in this case, hostin') shoes; off we go!

"Do not *volunteer* a visit to a friend in the country, or in another town, unless you have had what is called a standing invitation, with every reason to believe that it was sincerely and cordially given."

—If you try to invite yourself over to Miss Leslie's house, well, you've been warned.

INVITING THE *World*[*]
into your home
*Or at least the best parts of it.

As a homebody, I *love* having people over. It is the only place where my extroversion and mild agoraphobia can not only coexist but even dwell harmoniously. I don't know if I will like that bar, restaurant, or show. But you know what I *do* like? All the time? My house! And I want other people to like it, too. I want to have a house that feels comfy and happy, and that, when I look at the couch, I know that it tenderly holds the memory of each and every one of my loved ones' behinds.[note]

But it was not always this way! For years and years, I *did not want to have people over*, because that would require cleaning (as

---

Is this a *Simpsons* quote? I feel like it is, but couldn't confirm via Google.

Too much? Too much.

previously noted, "slob" is my natural setting; only through diligent, constant focus can I be otherwise), *and* I let great be the enemy of good.

I assumed that I could not have people over unless I knew that *every single detail was utter perfection.* I don't know what I thought would happen! I guess I figured that my friends who previously loved me would be so stricken by the use of paper, rather than fine linen napkins, that they would *swear off me forever.* Someone would open my fridge and see the weird dried-out condiment stains and that would be the beginning of the end. Word would spread about my failures as a hostess, and by extension as a human being.

I would be ejected and exiled from my own land, forced to live somewhere cold, like South Dakota, my only companions the stoic buffalo, and even they would snub me,🍍 at which point I would live in a sea cave.🍍🍍 Think pieces would be written; perhaps in time, my name would come to be shorthand for "someone who *thinks* they can do something and then fails spectacularly." If only I'd had those linen napkins!🍍🍍🍍

Then I got a better-paying job and linen napkins and *everything was perfect.* No, just kidding, though I do now have cloth napkins— thank you, IKEA's Last Chance aisle. I got over myself and realized that it's a sad thing not to have my favorite people in my favorite place, and they love me and aren't judgmental about any of the thousands of small details that I think they would.

If you approach entertaining as something you *have* to do in return for something, then you will resent putting forth the time,

🍍 As Wikipedia just now told me, you do *not* want to experience their "wild and ungovernable temper." Do go on, Wikipedia! "They can jump close to 6 feet (1.8 meters) vertically, and run 35 to 40 mph (56 to 64 km/h) when agitated." WHAT! *Buffalo can jump 6 damn feet in the air when agitated, which they **will** be, on account of those wild and ungovernable tempers!* What makes them maddest?

🍍🍍 I actually encountered a man—Lee Gray, the Wild Gourmet!—who had many tales of his time living in sea caves, and how he used to eat five sand dollars a day. I would be remiss not to share this with y'all.

🍍🍍🍍 These are, I assume, the kind of thoughts everyone has. Perfectly normal; perfectly healthy.

energy, and money that hosting implies. You will not have fun. In fact, probably no one but your very densest guests will. 🍍

But when you think of it as something you *get* to do, a gift you are giving to people whose very *existence* on this planet brings you gratitude and joy? It becomes a different animal entirely. 🍍🍍 I *get* to spend time sharing my very favorite things and thinking about what will bring my friends and family joy. That outlook transforms drudging to-dos into tiny acts of service toward a physical manifestation of my love, even if that love is just a cheese plate and a clean bathroom.

"I love to do a lot of work for my parties, because for me, it's a creative process . . . these are people you love coming to your home, and they're making an effort and this is like a gift you're giving them," said Mary Jane Murrell. "Your job when you're the host is to make people *feel* like the most special snowflake, just for a short time, because that's just a magical moment you can give someone. And how often do we get to feel like that?"

Not enough, Mary Jane! Not nearly enough.

Mary Jane and her daughter Nora are, to be fair, the most gifted hosts imaginable because they have spent a *lot* of time and energy practicing and perfecting. Every, every, everything takes practice, y'all, and if you don't have that practice then you probably won't stick the landing the first few times you go for that triple lutz. 🍍🍍🍍 Approach hosting with a clear set of priorities:

Priority 1: Making people feel loved and comfortable

Priorities 2 to 748: Redacted for space, but includes things like laughing and talking, sharing a convivial joy that y'all are together and there's food and this is *great*, introducing two

🍍 Bless their sweet, kind, dummy hearts.

🍍🍍 I'd say it transforms from an opossum to a tiny manatee—think about 4 inches long, very emotionally intelligent and always down to just listen without judgment, wearing a tiny top hat or fascinator every now and again. MANATEENY!

🍍🍍🍍 This is a thing, I believe, an ice-skating thing. Google can answer any further questions you may have on the topic.

friends who you think would love each other, making smart hats out of aluminum foil then wearing them because why not! 🍍

Priority 749: Ensuring that the roast is *perfectly rested* at the *ideal temperature* at 7:26 p.m., and *not a moment before!*

The great news here is that *most of the time* you have the most receptive and forgiving audience in the world, which is the people who love you and are here to have a nice time. They did not come to your house because they expect to have a meal worthy of Michelin stars, nor did they come to inspect whether each of the 17 flatware pieces are placed correctly. They came because you invited them and everyone's here for a good time. Serving the cheese at an incorrect temperature or using those darned paper napkins might haunt your dreams, but *nobody else is going to even register those things.*

Sure, you may have the occasional unpleasant relative, competitive colleague, or difficult friend-of-a-friend, but you always have the upper hand if you remember that *you're* the one feeding and entertaining them for free. If they expect to be treated like they're at French Laundry with Martha Stewart personally curating the experience, well, it's tough to live a life in which reality has zero bearing on your expectations. They can hopefully sort out those issues with the relevant professionals and just not accept your next invitation, should you even care to extend one. No *worthwhile* friend's night has *ever* been ruined because the beets were overcooked.

The night could be ruined, however, if you *make those ding-dang beets the sole topic of conversation and allow your hosting anguish and insecurities to wash over everyone.* In this case, the beets don't ruin the evening; your refusal to step away from your own insecurity does.

🍍 This is another Carol Kaplan innovation and it's great. Every New Year's Eve—or whenever the fancy strikes—just know that you can make great, great hats out of tinfoil. Give it a go some afternoon when you're feeling blue and need an insane pick-me-up. Remember: Be gentle and loose until the form is just right, and while you may certainly aim for a certain look, know that aluminum foil is a spirited medium, so don't be afraid to let it take the lead.

Remember that the tone of any party flows from the host, and every single human in the world would rather go to a party with burned beets and a happy host who makes them feel welcome than a flawless dinner served by someone who is clearly miserable.

So please, if you are just taking baby steps into entertaining and you read something in here and think, "Oh my God, you're supposed to do *that*?" then relax your anxious-acorn self. The only two things *truly* required to host people are:

1. Happiness that they have come over and you are together, and

2. A functioning toilet

Let us start with the smallest and easiest and build slooooowly up to the peaks of hospitality, which is to say: large social functions and long-term houseguests.

THE *Most Simple* HOSTING

Will go just like this:

1. Call a friend and ask if she or he wants to come over to hang out after work or on a weekend.

2. If necessary, go to store for bread, cheese, sweet things, and your friend's drink of choice.

3. Come home. Make certain that no underwear is visible in the home, and wash any dirty dishes, then . . .

4. Have a heart that is chock-full o' joy because someone likes you and you like them and you can talk or not talk

10 Exceptionally Basic Things to Have on Hand That Will Always Leave You Prepared for Someone to Stop By

- Iced tea in a pitcher in the fridge if it's above 40°F
- A decent selection of tea bags, with and without caffeine
- Honey
- Lemon
- Sparkling water
- Ice cubes
- Cookies
- Baby carrots
- Hummus
- Fruit

Voilà! These items will at least satisfy nearly every human in the world, regardless of unique dietary restrictions or personal preferences.

or watch a movie or complain about the world or work on your needlepoint or whatever it is that bonds you to this human.

That is the simplest compound that we build from. You have an invitation, refreshments, an activity of some sort that can be decided upon in the moment, and of course company. That's it! Technically, you don't need refreshments or activities; with the best of friends, you can just heat up leftovers and talk about nothing but also the *most important thing* for 5 hours.

Before the Festivities

Anytime you elevate beyond the "Hey, do you want to come over tonight?" deal, it's nice to give yourself at least a moment to plan.

So what shall we do? Have four people over for hot dogs and croquet on a sunny Saturday? Or 64 of your very best friends for a 14-course dinner? There is one thing that will always remain the same, that literally everyone I spoke to about this said, almost verbatim:

If you are going to cook (there's nothing wrong with takeout!), then *cook something you can cook well.*

Seriously! It could be the same menu every time! No one cares, and, in fact, it's sort of wonderful for people to know that every time they come over, they will get something they love.

When I was calling around scheduling interviews, I called a lovely woman named Ruth, and she said, "Oh! Well, you know, there is a lunch that I LOVE to make, so I'll make it for you, too!" and my heart grew two sizes at the idea of adorable Ruth at the grocery store knowing *just what to get for a luncheon.*

I *always* cook gumbo for people, because I know exactly how it will turn out and almost everyone likes it. Your signature move in the kitchen doesn't have to be fancy or exotic; all it has to be is tasty. If you make the best grilled cheese sandwich in the world, don't hide your humble yet perfect light! Also, everyone loves grilled cheese.

All right, now that that supremely important tidbit is on the table, let us move on to . . .

THE THEME

Not everything, of course, needs to be thematic. But thematic parties, I can say with the greatest of conviction, are *fun.*

"I like to think of a theme that I think is really wonderful, and

"However close your intimacy, an unexpected arrival may possibly produce inconvenience to your hostess; particularly if her family is numerous, or her bedchambers few."

—Miss Leslie reminds us to keep in mind whether the place we are visiting only has one bathroom.

I sort of go from there," Mary Jane said, adding quickly that not *every* party has to have a theme. Some of the most fun and easiest get-togethers she throws are just inviting everyone over to do a craft—say, carving pumpkins around Halloween or making Valentines together—then she just gets some wine and orders enough pizza for everyone.

But for the more complicated soirees, "The thing that saves my life are sticky notes, and I have them *all* over my bathroom mirror—every time I have an idea, I write it on a sticky note, and then I throw away the sticky notes that are not the greatest ideas.

"Do anything you can do; stick to your strengths," was her recommendation for any hosting efforts, big or small. "If you want to put a little flower arrangement together, cut a few branches down, put them in a vase, and that makes it look special," she said. "Anything you can think of that makes this person feel special—a bottle of wine you've enjoyed together before, rolling up the hand towels in the bathroom and doing a spa spread, having some beautiful soaps. You don't have to be that creative—just put the effort in."

This, as you may have gathered, is quite a bit of work for Mary Jane because she tends toward elaborate gestures, but she doesn't mind.

"I do a lot of work for these parties, and I love it—for me, it's a creative process and I just feel like these people are coming to your house, they're taking the time and making the effort, and this is a gift you're giving them."

THE Guest List

But who shall be receiving these gifts? There are the parties where everyone knows everyone (and if you host enough, this will happen no matter how many groups of friends you have! It's the best!) and the parties designed to introduce friends to one another.

I like to think about a mix of both, and the first question is how many? There is an inverse relationship that can and should be at play between the number of guests and the intensive-detail factor, at least while you're getting your host legs under you.🍍 It is really easy to have a couple over for dinner, because I can just double whatever I'm making. I don't worry too much about even vs. odd groups, or about couples vs. singles, particularly if everyone knows everyone else, but that sneaky move of inviting two single friends you suspect would really enjoy each other is always aces. Please be extra aware of your single friends and extend the invite; a lot of times, they are left off the guest list and, having been in that position myself, I can say with authority that it sucks to feel like your friends care less if your life circumstances alter their heretofore perfect seating chart. Finally, how many cups do you have?

A few principles I've found convenient:

🍍 I like to make sure that everyone has previously met and had a good conversation with at least one other person at the party that they are not in a relationship with. An exception here can be ultra-gregarious friends *or* people who are new in town and looking to meet folks. In this case, I will share with you a hosting secret called the sorority-style bump (see page 149) that will be extra crucial.

🍍 Does anyone on this list not wish to see someone else on the list? This happens a lot with former couples or former friends. The first option would be to pick one this time and one next time. The other option, if it's a large enough gathering, is to invite both and let each know that the other is invited, then let everyone be a grown-up and make their own decisions.

🍍 Do you owe anyone an invitation? That is to say, has someone hosted you and you've yet to return the favor?

🍍 Is there anyone who would feel like they were *specifically* not invited if they heard the guest list? If so, why are they not on it? Not to say that you *need* to invite them, but if you have five

🍍 Like sea legs, just maintaining verbal and logistical balance no matter how high the swells

close girlfriends and normally it's the six of y'all but someone is not on the list, be prepared for hurt feelings.

🐚 It's okay to issue an invitation that you are guessing someone cannot accept due to distance or scheduling difficulties, but know there is always that chance that they may show up.

Invitations!

Written invitations are always delightful, because then people can put them on their fridge and get excited. Those fill-in-the-blank invitations are fine (*I suppose* [sorry, not sure why I'm being a jerk about this, except that stationery is literally the only thing in the world I'm a snob about]) BUT! Something just as fast and much more fun is a postcard.

If you'd like, e-mail invitations are good, too, as are texts, or even better, calling the person to invite them, *then* texting the details so it's in writing. I'd say that social media (Facebook!) invitations imply a certain level of casualness and you never know whether someone will see it or not. This kind of invitation is best for really large gatherings that don't have a head count restriction but also that won't be awkward if the majority of your invitees don't come.

Do *let everyone know exactly where and when this party is happening.* Be so crystal clear. If they've RSVP'd yes, great! Call them and say you're so excited, then ask if they have any food likes or dislikes. This allows everyone to recite whatever their dietary restrictions may be. This is *also* a great way to round up the nonresponsive—"Hello! I don't know whether you'll be able to make it to my Leap Day brunch, but just in case, I wanted to check in and ask . . . "

If those requests have to do with serious allergies/truly over-the-top diets/impossible-to-cook-anything-that-other-guests-would-enjoy guidelines, you can say, "You know, I'm dying to have you come be with us, but I just can't guarantee that my kitchen is salt-, flour-, sugar-, fat- and electron-free. Are there any restaurants nearby that

CARTE POSTALE

Darling Lelia—
Can you and Cole
make it to dinner
at 8 p.m. on
Saturday Aug 6.
at my house? Let
me know!
xoxo Kelly

Ms Lelia Gowland
811 Fancy Lady
Boulevard
New Orleans LA

have something you like that I could pick up and keep separate and
safe? No, *please*! I insist! It wouldn't be the same without you, but I
would just hate to serve you anything that doesn't agree with you."

Make sure that you know when people are coming. If they ask
whether they can bring something, I'll usually say that a bottle of
wine is always great. If they are one of those wonderful people who
like to bake and make dessert, then a dessert can be a nice ask, too.

About 2 days before party time is a great time to start reluctantly (if you are me) tidying up and thinking about time lines, generally. Do you have all the supplies that you need? Have you hit up the grocery store yet or figured out what you'll be purchasing when you go? Maybe go ahead and do that, too.

"Having received an invitation, reply to it immediately; and do not keep your friends waiting, day after day, in uncertainty whether you mean to accept or decline it, causing them, perhaps, to delay asking other visitors till they have ascertained if you are to be expected or not."

—Miss Leslie finds the second-tier invite totally acceptable.

"The key is doing food that you can make ahead of time, food that you know you're good at making—don't try to do any surprise recipes. Make the same thing over and over once you know it's going to turn out," Mary Jane said. "You can even do it the day before! And that way, all you have to worry about is getting the house and yourself ready the day of."

If indeed it *is* the day of, I like to take a tip from Ina Garten[*] and sketch out the day ahead in the morning. First, figure out what time you want to serve dinner, then count backward from there, taking into account how long each component will take. You'll get something like this:

7:30 p.m.: DINNER! Roast, potatoes, and salad.

7:25 p.m.: Potatoes come out of oven.

7:15 p.m.: Roast comes out of oven for 15-minute rest.

7:00 p.m.: Guests arrive.

6:50 p.m.: Put out dip, chips, bread, and salsa.

6:40 p.m.: Prep potatoes and put in oven.

6:30 p.m.: Shave cheese on salad, make vinaigrette.

5:15 p.m.: Put on makeup, brush hair, watch *30 Rock*.

5:00 p.m.: Make smoked salmon dip.

4:10 p.m.: Set the table.

4:00 p.m.: Put roast in oven.

3:30 p.m.: Prep roast.

Then type it out into a schedule, and voilà! No more wondering when you should put the potatoes in. It's *on the ding-dang schedule!*

Do not forget to give yourself time to get ready, *and* make sure to

Hail, BAREFOOT CONTESSA, GODDESS OF OUR HEARTS! INA! HAIL!

include a little extra time for doing whatever it is that you love to do, hosting-wise.

Some people are phenomenal cooks. Other people love doing crafts and making little name cards for everyone. Some people, who are Nora, make *adorable cheese balls with tiny almond slivers stuffed in them that look like hedgehogs*. Whatever element you enjoy doing, make *that* the focus of the evening, and make sure that anything else you've decided to include is low maintenance.

During

Repeat after me: *The tone of the party flows from the host. The tone of the party flows from the host.* THE TONE OF THE PARTY FLOWS FROM . . . WHAT? Yes. Host. Correct. Sorry.

It is so important to not let great be the enemy of good when you're hosting an event. It's as much your job to relax and to enjoy yourself as it is to make sure that the big stuff is taken care of. If whatever form of hosting you're doing is simply so taxing that you cannot summon a single bit of calm and happy behavior, then I'm afraid you are entertaining above your pay grade, and I say good for you! Now you know, and there's *nothing wrong with being ambitious and trying new things*. Plus, it is an AFGO: You will remember this experience next time you think of having your 50 closest friends over for a 14-course dinner in honor of your pug Agatha's fourth birthday.

"The best thing you can do as a hostess is go around to each guest and have a meaningful conversation with them—make sure they know you're so excited to have them in your home and treat them as though they are the most interesting, wonderful person they've ever met," Mary Jane said.

Hold up, Mary Jane. Is everyone you know really this incredibly exciting and fascinating?

She laughed. "Sometimes yes, sometimes no," she said. "Sometimes you fake it! That's the kind thing to do."

Once everyone has arrived and the drinks have not yet kicked in

Another F***ing Growth Opportunity

and things are a little bit awkward because . . . well, they just are. In these times, I revert to my sorority days. During rush (excuse me: *potential new member recruitment*) parties, we did something called bumping that is as socially calculated as can be *and* quite effective. *Essentially, by doing a little bit of research and calculation ahead of time, we could make sure that strangers had something meaty in common to talk about, which can kick off a conversation that then flows naturally.*

To any young ladies who are soon to go through sorority recruitment, the slightly creepy news is that *the sororities know everything about you already.* Yeah. They know what high school you went to, what your extracurriculars are, what you're majoring in—basically everything you put down on that little form when you registered, plus your Instagram.

Here's how bumping goes: Let's say I am positively *dying* to have Josie in the sorority. I know that she's from LA, she is majoring in psychology, and she loves red pandas because she's a human being with blood in her veins.

So I am chatting away with darling Josie, and then all of a sudden, Erin approaches.

"Oh!" I say, turning to Erin as though her appearance is a surprise and not one step in a terrifically choreographed ballet that has taken *months* to prepare. "Erin! This is Josie. Josie, this is my lovely sister Erin—Erin, you're a psych major, right? So is Josie! Josie, do you know what field you want to go into?"

And then Josie will talk about her dreams of opening the Red-Panda Therapy for Nervous Ladies Center of Excellence,🍍 and Erin will smile and talk about *her* plans to train emotional comfort foxes that can tell when you're getting anxious and do some frolicking🍍🍍—they are off to the races. *Meanwhile,* it is time for me to go relieve Elisabeth of the girl from Oregon who, like me, was a speech nerd in high school.

🍍 Someone please start this; I will give you a very large percentage (72) of my money.

🍍🍍 Science, are you listening?

A FEW THINGS TO THINK ABOUT WHEN MAKING SMALL TALK

1. Back in the old sorority days, we were often reminded to not mention the six B's during sorority recruitment: Bodies, Bush (George W.), the Bible, Bank Accounts, Boys, or Booze. Now! No one ever likes talking about their own body—anyone's bodies, really. Politics can be terribly tricky. Religion, you know, God lives in your heart or not, and that is a conversation that requires closeness and respect on both sides. When it comes to money, you never, ever know someone's financial situation and shouldn't make assumptions. Boys, we weren't to discuss on the chance that we had hooked up with the same guy as this Potential New Member (it was a very small, very gender-lopsided campus, and the ratio was not in our favor); I guess the lesson for small talk would be to not give a recitation of your recent *lovers*. 🍍 Booze, well . . . I guess y'all can talk about it. But *not* in a way that is trying to impress upon younger people that you're the *coolest* because all y'all drink *sooooo* much. This is strictly verboten.

2. Never underestimate the power of questions! Be curious about their lives; listen closely to answers and then ask follow-ups.

3. An important note to go with the above: Be careful about not seizing on an answer that broadcasts some amount of personal pain. If someone mentions that their friend has died, "Oh my goodness, I am so, so sorry to hear that. That is just awful," is the correct response, not "What happened?"

🍍 Attn. Anne C.: This use of the word "lover"—all of them, really—are in this book just to irk you. That's how much I love you. Lovahhhh.

What can we learn here, beyond "sororities are equal parts amazing and terrifying"?

- Know ahead of time what your guests have in common—and it doesn't have to be, like, "Hey, you both are super into this very obscure hobby!" so much as "Hey, you both watch X show and I know that so I'm going to ask one of you if you're up on it."

- People usually appreciate a little something to get started on, some tiny square yard of common ground. From there, they can go wherever they like!

- As the host, once they start talking about the *Game of Thrones* deaths and whether Kip (Ted? Birnk? Something One-Syllable) Snow is *actually* beheaded and oh, man, wasn't it rough when *literally every character everyone likes plus all the diredogs were systematically sliced to pieces in a 45-minute slow motion montage,* 🍍 then it's your cue to smile, lightly touch one of them on the shoulder, and say, "I'm off to check on the roast!" so that you may go bump your next guest.

If you've invited people over for a meal, it's a pretty good idea to serve them sooner rather than later. I've been at parties where it's been more than 2 hours before anything but crudités materialize, and one can only be sustained with baby carrots for so long.

Whoever is going to be going back and forth to the kitchen most frequently should sit at the head of the table, closest to the kitchen.

When it comes to serving, a buffet spread where everyone serves themselves is a lot simpler than serving, especially since it's so hard to find a good footman these days. Wait for a slight lull in the conversation, and then brightly say, "Well, dinner is ready! [Whoever is at that moment standing closest to the buffet but isn't paralyzingly shy, in which case person who is standing second-closest to the buffet], do you want to grab one of those plates and get started?"

🍍 I have spent a lot of time listening to friends talk about *Game of Thrones*. This is the extent of my understanding.

Many of us, in the most secret place in our heart, want to go through the buffet first but are ashamed. What makes us worthy of scooping our mashed potatoes 20 seconds before anyone else gets to scoop theirs? By specifically nominating someone, you spare guests this question of self-worth, which usually translates to everyone milling around with their plates but no one actually *going through the damn line.*

If you're last through the line, some people at the table may be waiting for you. Some people may even be *standing behind their chairs if their mamma raised them right!* In this case, if you don't want that kind of pressure, trill cheerfully from the kitchen: "Please go ahead! I'll be there in 90 seconds!"

Munch munch munch. Eat eat eat. If there's more than one course, wait until the slowest eater is within a minute of finishing, then ask if you can clear the plate of the person who was done 20 minutes ago.

Wow. What a wondrous party that was! The food! The laughter! The friendship! The board gaming! The alcohol! Wow. As was written so memorably in a yearbook about that year's Sadie Hawkins dance, *friends were made.*

But now, it is time for friends to go, because you're pretty tuckered out. Again, some people will feel uncomfortable about being the first to leave, and yet no one wants to live in your living room.

Some good "please get out" signs include, but are not limited to:

- Vague murmurs about what a wonderful evening it has *been* because now we're not present tense, y'all, this party is *past tense.*

- Lovingly rubbing your significant other's back and saying quietly, "Are you sleepy, darling? You can go lie down."

"Excuse yourself from accepting invitations from persons whom you do not like, and whose dispositions, habits, feelings, and opinions are in most things the reverse of your own."

—Miss Leslie gives the best description of Donald Trump I've ever read.

❀ Relaying how excited you are for that marathon tomorrow! Oh, you've been training and you can't *wait*. But eesh, that 6:00 a.m. start time!

Hopefully, everyone will take the hint. If someone has had too much fun (read: alcohol), definitely beg them to stay overnight if that's possible and if not, beg them to let you call them a taxi and you'll pick them up in the morning to fetch their car. Start with cajoling, then move slowly but surely into, "No, really, this is what's happening now," mode. This can be a very, very tough situation but, let us remember, *safety always trumps politeness*. So stand firm.

Houseguests

Oh, they are a delight! Sort of! It can be tough, though, and sometimes, particularly if you live in a city that people like to visit, you will find yourself inundated with offers from people who are *so very willing to stay in your house for free*.

Never forget that the bigger the ask—and there is very little bigger than, "Hey, can I come be in your only private space in the world day in, day out?"—the more comfortable you can be in turning it down.

"Oh, I'd love to, but we'll be out of town that week."

"Oh, I'd love to, but that month is going to be nuts at work, and I'd hate not to get to spend time with you."

"Oh, I'd love to, but we've already got plans that fortnight."

"Oh, I'd love to. But I can't."

Those are listed in ascending order of the would-be guest's inability to take a damn hint.

When you *do* want someone to come, *make that very apparent*. Don't make a vague future offering—"Oh, you should come visit me in New Orleans!" unless you *actually want them to stay with you*. If you would love them to see your city, but you do not want them in your space, a much more accurate statement would be "Oh, you really should see New Orleans. Let me know next time you'll be in town, and I'd love to play tour guide for a day!"

THE MOST *Miraculous* HOUSEGUEST EXPERIENCE *Ever!*

If you are wondering how to host someone, WELL. Take a knee, boys, and let me tell you a story. 🍍

My friend Jessica Maxwell is . . . oh, gosh, how do I describe Jessica? She and I had one of those love-at-first-sight-except-friendship moments when I did a Sunday profile on her. Like me, she's a redheaded Leo writer who is very into spirituality (I'll let her speak for herself on the matter, as she did so beautifully in her book *Roll Around Heaven*) but ALSO wants to spend, say, no less than 2 hours discussing the virtues of a particular vintage pink Chinoise loveseat. I am obsessed with her.

Anyway, one time I was in town and happened to knock on Jessica's door, because that is sort of how I do with her. She answered the beautiful door to her home, Gaiety Hill House, a stunning, sprawling 1930s Colonial Revival that is full of art and beautiful furniture and back staircases and silver tea services.

"*Darling!* Kelly! *Darling Kelly!* I can't BELIEVE it, I was JUST thinking about you, and—oof, you know, I am *right* in the middle of a spiritual clearing with a client, but *what are you doing here? Where are you staying? A couch?* Oh, no, no, dear. No, no, no. You MUST stay here, you simply *must.*"

Obviously, the fact that Jessica speaks like Katharine Hepburn and *isn't* doing it on purpose is one of the 10,000 things I love about her.

So off I went, into her guest suite, which was, in fact, larger than my house.

Y'allllllllllll, this room. I cannot describe this room. It is her

---

🍍 Obviously that was in the voice of Coach Taylor from *Friday Night Lights*. In fact, until I say otherwise, just pretend that all of is this being said either by Coach or Tami Taylor. Or both, in calm, reassuring unison, right before you have a three-way with them.

Healing Room, which means it's full of hydrangea blossoms and altars and smells like a dream and has huge, vaulted ceilings and a bed full of squishy pillows. That room is everyyyyyyything, every single thing in the world. Line up all the things, count 'em—this room wins every time.

However! The point of this story is *not* that you should track Jessica down and trick her into liking you and letting you stay in the Healing Room, though I would recommend that highly.

The room would've been enough to floor me. But! It also contained *literally everything that a weary traveler could ever want.*

On each side of the bed was a bedside table, with bowls containing:

- Two sleep masks
- Lavender essential oil
- Melatonin tablets, in case you couldn't sleep
- Over-the-counter pain reliever
- A small flashlight, so that if you needed something in the middle of the night, you wouldn't wake up anyone who happened to be sleeping in the bed next to you
- Packets of Emergen-C
- Breath mints

I knooooow. But it didn't stop there! On or near the bed, there were:

- Slippers
- A robe
- A power strip tucked discreetly under the bedside table

Jessssssica, stop it! No one deserves this, least of all a last-minute unexpected guest! But Jessica neither could nor would stop. Spread out for me on a beautiful sofa was:

- A note welcoming me
- A sweet gift (she keeps lots of these around for such occasions; in this case, she gave me darling hand-knit alpaca hand warmers *because I have typing to do*)

- A dress she didn't wear much that she thought I would love because she knows I adore navy and polka dots and dressing like a teenager from 1963

And oh, God, *the bathroom.* What is in the bathroom, laid out in perfect formation?

- A gentle cleansing facial mask
- A nonbreakable but beautiful water glass
- Toothbrush and toothpaste, in a tiny kit
- A shower cap
- Cotton balls
- Floss
- Contact lens solution
- A razor

My guess, when she was setting those things out, she did not know how awful my day had been, and that all those things would make me burst into tears of love and gratitude and wonder how many thousands of orphans and kittens I saved in a previous life to deserve her as a friend.

We cannot all be Jessica, though I shall spend the rest of my life trying. We can, however, take some lessons. Those items set by the bed? Fantastic, and I will never again have a houseguest without setting out some kind of basket like that.

I think about what kinds of things I tend to forget when I'm traveling and make sure that I have some extra travel-size quantities of them stashed away—toothbrushes and travel-size deodorants are true lifesavers when you need them. I think about what kinds of questions I usually have when I'm in someone else's home and try to make those answers available. (Hint: A cute framed picture with the WiFi network and password on it and extra blankets that can be easily accessed–this is how you host like a pro champion, y'all.)

And you don't have to run out to the nearest spa to stock up whenever you're going to have a houseguest for the weekend. Just keep your eyes open and gather the supplies you need as you encounter them, like when you're in a hotel with bath products or notice that there's a sale on your favorite shampoo.

As for the gifts? Well, Jessica just keeps some gifts around! Why not? So now, when I am in a store, and I see a lovely $15 themed notepad/ceramic jewelry bowl/miniature bonsai tree/deep *tea* diver tea strainer that I technically don't need but want or think almost any of my friends would enjoy, I'm going to snatch it up.

Jessica Maxwell, ladies and gentlemen! Jessica Maxwell.

WHEN *you* ARE *hosted*

It *seems* like being hosted is much easier than hosting, because hey, all you have to do is show up! But, as my former mediocre yoga teacher self would remind my Salem YMCA pupils, if you are doing Mountain Pose (normally known as standing) correctly, then it should exhaust you pretty quickly—*at first!* Same with being hosted.

Just as your body will adjust to the noble nuances of *tadasana* and soon it will be a resting position, so too shall you be able to fully celebrate the positively *wonderful* circumstances that:

1. Someone likes you enough to *have you over! Maybe for more than a few hours, or days,* when they could be watching

(continued on page 160)

Also, I would be remiss not to mention her husband, Tom Andersen, who is also a host extraordinaire—affable, charming and quite graceful despite clocking in at 6 foot 4. Tom is 97 percent as wonderful as Jessica is—as he put it: "In absolute terms, I'm pretty nice. Compared to Jessica, though . . ." and I noted that she does *totally* ruin the bell curve. Tom is a silver-fox city council member, and I could watch the two of them interact for years and not get even slightly bored.

" . . . balancing your weight over both feet, tailbone reeeeaching toward the ground, liiiiiiiifting your thighs up and backward, letting them be strong but keeping your belly soft, like the teeniest, tiniest baby koala's tum. Innnnnnnnn-hale deeply, close your eyes and envision – see and know that *you* are that baby koala's tummy, so full of eucalyptus-scented milk. Just an egoless stomach, connected to all, *turgid* with koala breast milk. Exhale, letting all that milk flow out of you. Make your mind still, gently dismiss thoughts and emotions as they arise without judgment. . . . Did you know that sometimes they try to get BACK in their mom's pouch, but won't fit? The baby koalas, I mean. Doesn't that seem like a metaphor for life, somehow? Let's ponder that as we exxxxxhale and fold forward . . . "

WHEN YOU ARE HOSTING…A *LOVER!*

I'm so sorry about that heading but I could not help myself. I mostly did it to annoy my friend Anne and all those like her, who involuntarily pull their entire head backward when that word comes up.

Anyway! Let us say you have an overnight guest for whom you do not need to put fresh sheets on the guest bed . . . but who is not a regular presence at your home.

This is very important: *We all should be more, not less, polite to the people we are close to.* The principle is obvious when it comes to friends, but it can sometimes get lost when we think about romantic partners, or families. Or people we are physically but maybe not emotionally close to.

If you've decided this human is charming and wonderful and attractive enough to come in your home (and you are 100 percent sure they are not a serial killer; I'm not trying to be a killjoy but please be safe, y'all), then they are your guest and need to be treated courteously.

Go in with the assumption that they will want to spend the night. If you really can't stand the very idea of waking up to them, then maybe have that particular assignation somewhere that is not your bed? Or even reconsider the entire arrangement?

They will want to take a shower, and if you can offer them a toothbrush, I feel like that's in everyone's best interest.

It's nice, when you're issuing an invitation (or enlarging the scope of an already-existing invitation) to be *very clear what the invitation is and is not for.* Any worthy ~~lover~~ temporary houseguest will pay very strict attention to those invitations and not overstep. If they don't, that makes them an *ungracious* temporary houseguest and is grounds for immediate expulsion.

In general, be on your best behavior when it comes to having sex with someone (well, in certain ways, anyway). Pay attention to where they are emotionally, as well as where you are emotionally, and make sure those two outlooks are congruent enough that no one is getting damaged. Treat them however they want inside the bedroom and with consideration, respect, and honesty outside of it.

Sexuality is a beautiful and wonderful and terrifying thing, and if we're not careful with it, we can really, really hurt people, first and foremost ourselves. Back to the practical, fun tips!

- If you are ever strapped for a delightful and quick postcoital meal, may I suggest carbonara? All you need is pasta, eggs, Parmesan, and some sort of fatty pork (pancetta, bacon—I've even used prosciutto and tasso and straight-up deli ham). The *New York Times* has the perfect recipe for it.

- A pitcher of water, plus a glass for you and whomever may also be in need of hydration, is great.

- Be clear about your morning plans, and what time you will be leaving. They should know, unless you specify otherwise, that they need to leave *before* then. If you don't mind them sleeping in, do let them know of any locking-up protocol.

- Follow up the same way you might with a friend after a fun get-together. "So lovely to see you, as always! Hope you have a fantastic Wednesday, [flattery and or fond reminiscing that would embarrass my mother redacted here]."

- Finally, because I haven't gotten it in the book anywhere else, my favorite dirty joke:

    Q: Why don't Southern girls do orgies?

    A: Too many thank-you notes.

Netflix and eating pastry! Instead, they looked inside their heart and found the desire to host you, which means they will spend time, effort, and money on . . .

2. Feeding you, entertaining you, making you feel comfortable, talking to you, listening to your thoughts, laughing at your jokes, thinking about your pleasures and preferences, watching your water glass so that you do not dehydrate on their watch, fetching you a new cold or adult drink🍍/the next course/fresh towels for your shower, and let's not forget that . . .

3. They will even wash your dirty dishes.

The *first* step is remembering all of the above. The second step is retracing those mental steps again through a new filter.

"When I think of someone who's gracious, I think of them as always being thankful—no one owes you anything," Nora said. "If someone invites you to a party, that's an *amazing thing!* It's not like you are *entitled* to go to that party, so you don't complain about it to them or anyone else, and you don't wish that the party was different or think about the ways you could do it better. You are just unbelievably grateful that someone other than your parents or your significant other thought enough of you to invite you to an event that's important to them, to specifically want *you* there."

Yesssss, brave yet darling pelicans, now we are in the right state of mind! But best visiting practices begin *long* before you ring the doorbell or cross that threshold.

First, you have RSVP'd as soon as you possibly can and, if you are *legitimately* unsure of whether or not you can come because

🍍 As you may have picked up by now, I'm a retired drunk, as my rehab friend Tom said. He has the world's most charming New Zealand accent, which I will totally butcher here as I spell it phonetically: "Oi mean, believe yew me, Oi did it with the best of 'em! Many hoigh-level accolaydes! And achiv'mints! But Oi've hung up mah jersey, I told the boys the other night! And they thought I was putting one on! . . . (quieter) But Oi was *quite seriahhzs.*" Oh my God, Tom, if you're reading this, *I miss you.*

AN *Excellent* WAY TO *decline*

Sometimes, you just do *not* want to go to something. That's okay! Unless that thing is a baby shower or funeral because obviously no one wants to go to those but we do anyway.

If you are someone who is not comfortable saying, "Oh, I'm sorry, I won't be able to make it," which is a *perfectly valid* way to decline, then try this: "Oh, I'm sorry! I actually have plans with my family that night."

No one ever need know that here, you are counting *yourself* as your family ⚬ and your plans are to spend the evening as you please rather than attending something you'd rather not.

🍍 If you are not your own family, *then I would like to know who is,* missy or mister!

you might be getting a new kidney that night, then you either let them know just as soon as you possibly can or gratefully decline the invitation and give a brief summation of the circumstances.

"Oh, my goodness, I would *absolutely love* to attend tiny Trevin's preschool graduation gala, but I'm afraid that night is going to be tough, because there's a 10 percent chance that I will be having major lifesaving surgery, and I won't know until a day or so ahead of time! I would hate to cancel at the last minute. Please, enjoy some of those fabulous Cheerio cocktails for me!"

Now, at this point, your would-be host might say, "Oh, you know, it just wouldn't be the same without you and it's a totally casual white-tie gala for 400 people, so why don't we plan on you coming and if you can't make it, just let me know the day of?"

In this case, I hope you *really are getting that kidney and not just using it as an excuse* because you can't back out! Please see flaking chart on page 217.

In the event that you actually *can't or sincerely don't want to*

KNOW *who's invited*

If the invite specified "and Guest" *or* it said somewhere that significant others are welcome, all is well. If Significant Other *wasn't* specifically invited *and* this feels like an oversight, you may make a passing reference to their existence during this phone call and hope the host picks up on it and issues the invite, but that's about it. Or, say something so casual—"Trevinka, I'm such a dingbat, but did you want Kyle to come with me or shall I go stag?" Otherwise: Invitations are for the person they are addressed to. The one exception is if you have a dear friend or relation in town for a very short while and the host knows them *or* would like to know them, then you can say, "You know, So-and-so is staying with me that weekend. I'm so sorry to ask and of course feel free to say no, but would there be room for them to come along with me?"

go, stick with the above script, replacing the "because there's a 10 percent chance . . . ahead of time!" bit with " . . . and I just can't make it." This conveys everything one needs to say when declining an invitation. If you are hoping for an invite in the future, it's a good idea to make sure that the host knows that this is *positively killing you* and you just *can't stand to miss this* and maybe even send *a stupid expensive Baby Industrialist-to-Be's First Paper Shredder* as a gift.

If you do want this person as part of your life, but that night doesn't work (and/or the idea of passed baby carrot hors d'oeuvres are just too much but you DO love this friend), make sure to invite *them* to something in the future, perhaps even on the same phone call—"I would just *love* to take you and Trevin out to lunch, and afterward we can visit the stock exchange! Oh my gosh, we haven't done that with him since he was, what, 3½? That was, oh my gosh, 6 months ago! I can't *believe* it's been that long! How does early August look for y'all?"

If, of course, you don't want to be friends with them, then it is just fine to decline the invitation. An obligatory friendship is not, technically speaking, a friendship, and gently but consistently turning down invitations is one way to wind things to a minimally hurtful close.

Let's say you can and will attend and are already trying to figure out which of your gowns will most gaily flutter in a bouncy castle. Stupendous! In this case, your RSVP—whether it be verbal, on Facebook/eVite/etc., or even by mail—*should convey your gratitude.*

"Trevinka?🍍 Yes! Significant Other and I will *definitely* be there, we are *so* excited, and please, what can I bring? Maybe some of those truffle-scented Teddy Grahams that Trevin likes so much?"🍍🍍

See, here you are suggesting something you can do rather than forcing the host to think of what they'd like to assign you, something that isn't *too* much to ask for but *is* in your wheelhouse and, ahh, would that be a burden? No, okay, they definitely shouldn't ask for that! Spare them that complicated, on-the-spot calculation.

Now, Trevinka may say, no, no, no, just your beautiful faces. *This is a lie!* Not that Trevinka is lying (though, now that I'm thinking about it, that *is* very Trevinka), but remember this: When you come to someone's house, it is *always* nice to arrive with a little something. That is never inappropriate!

You could, as I sometimes do, roll around with a decent bottle of wine *safely secured in your trunk* for times when you totally forget and don't want to show up empty-handed. If it's a little teeny-tiny get-together with a close girlfriend, then, duh, you

🍍 This is Trevin's mom. I haven't introduced her yet. But her name is Trevinka.

🍍🍍 If you really must, you can say "likes so *well.*" I won't judge.

SOME PERFECTLY WONDERFUL HOSTESS GIFTS UNDER $5

- A single big round flower in a little dollar-store bud vase
- A sweet card for them—encouraging if they're down, celebratory if it's a happy day, or one that will make them laugh if it's a just-because visit
- A cheese wedge (this may just be me, but I am never sorry to receive cheese of any kind)
- A used copy of a book you think they'd enjoy—bonus points if you write an inscription
- If you are an artsy or crafty person, maybe just a little tiny thing you drew/doodled/lettered/made for them
- If you are a cooking/baking person, a treat of some sort. Actually, if it's a one-on-one visit, why not swing by a local pastry place and grab a nice-looking tart or some macaroons?

don't *have* to get a gift. But, as stated before: Graciousness is not about what we have to do. It's about what we can do that shows love, attention, and kindness to those around us, especially those we love.

If I am traveling to stay with or visit someone, I like to bring them something from *my* home that they can't get. In Portland's case, this might be Stumptown coffee, or a liqueur from one of the microdistilleries, or any of the whimsical white people ephemera Portland is so renowned for. And, when I'm on my way home, it's *also* very, very nice to bring souvenirs—particularly for the people who have facilitated your journey by watching your house or your pet or transporting you to or from the airport or hurricane-proofing your house in the event of a freak storm—something small that you know they'd like is pretty much the least you can do.

Souvenirs!

... for places they don't remember. Because they weren't there.

I absolutely love bringing people little souvenirs, because then, when I'm on a trip, I get to *think* about them and what they would enjoy or not enjoy in that place, not to mention that I get to purchase smaller items that I *really* cannot justify buying for myself but bring me joy. The more distant the destination, the more this applies. However, to be successful, a souvenir must *actually be something that person would want or use,* and not just something that says the name of the place on it.

Costume jewelry, neat tiny arts or crafts, something tasty that customs won't confiscate—*perfect!* A sweatshirt or shot glass that says BILOXI in giant letters? Maybe not *quite* as perfect, unless this person has again and again demonstrated that there is truly nothing in the world that they want more than shot glasses with names of places on them, in which case, your job is easy!

Party Time!

How shall we behave?

Ah, the day has finally arrived when all gather to celebrate Trevin! In his short 39 months, he's done so much, and now that he got into that kindergarten, the future is so bright that even if he *didn't* have crippling sun and cloud allergies, he would *still* wear shades! Let us be our best selves for dear (gluten-, lactose-, nightshade-, star-, smile-intolerant) Trevin!

Day of: Do you have a hostess🍍 gift? Cool.

3 hours before: If you really absolutely MUST FLAKE OUT because that kidney came in, this is the cutoff time barring major emergencies.

🍍 No idea why this particular phrase is still gendered, but it's not a perfect world we live in, eh la la.

Hour before: Is everything set for you to arrive on time? If not, do text your hostess and let her know you'll be late, and by how much. Up to 15 minutes late to a dinner party is sort of customary and doesn't require a text. If you are bringing food, please make sure that it is securely packed and has a serving implement with it.

30 minutes before: All dressed and on your way? Wunderbar! It's nice to text and ask if they want you to pick up ice or anything.

Time of invitation: You may arrive at this time but *not a moment before*—unless you have asked the host if they would like your help cooking or decorating, which is always a nice and fun thing to do *and* ensures you get some one-on-one time.

Some hosts⸎ have an *exceptionally* intense last 15 minutes before the party because that's usually when I remember that while the food, drinks, decorations, and house are all ready to go, *I* am wearing fleece pants and have gravy in my hair and also on 40 percent of my face and need to remedy that situation. So, be on time if you must, but *nevuhhhh* before.

Ringing the doorbell . . . pausing . . . pretending not to hear whatever you may have heard shouted as the host approaches the door, annnnnd:

"Helloooooo! Oh my gosh, we are *so excited!*"

Now. At this moment, you probably have some things in your hands because you are about to hand them over. Our immediate response, upon seeing the person we will be handing something to, is to *do it right then and there.* As soon as you are within arms' length, thrust it right toward them.

However, it is *nice* to get all the way inside before even mentioning these things, so as not to display that sort of panicky "Ahhhh, all the things are so precarious, the center cannot hold, ahhhh!" body language. This may necessitate two trips to the car, which is better for everyone than loading every arm, wrist, and finger to maximum capacity.

🍍 Me.

POSTING ON SOCIAL MEDIA: MAYBE, DON'T, ALWAYS? OR AT LEAST DO IT THOUGHTFULLY

It is a sad but true fact that no matter how much we want to, we cannot invite everyone to everything. Back in the day, people were more respectful about not mentioning a party to someone else unless they were *positive* they were coming. Otherwise you could end up with someone—maybe, let's just say, me in fourth grade—up crying all night because *everyone is over at Jennifer S.'s birthday sleepover except for me and they are bedazzling things without me which I know because that's all anyone talked about all week and on Monday I will have to see all the bedazzled fanny packs.*

Jennifer, I forgive you. And all of us have had a lot to forgive over the years because with social media, it's a lot harder to keep social events private.

Please don't post from a smaller event unless you've checked with your host; if you are the host, it's perfectly fine to convey, quietly, at some point that because you couldn't invite everyone you wanted to, you'd prefer if pictures of the event could be kept off social media *or* weren't labeled. When you do post, use discretion—there's a difference between noting that you're 100 percent *feeling* this beef Wellington or a photo of you and one other friend together, versus a group shot of everyone who is at the table. In that second scenario, there are almost certainly some people who would like to be at that table but aren't, and you never know when feelings will be unintentionally hurt. Be extra careful about posting things when people are traveling; you have no idea if they want the world to know their whereabouts.

AN Excellent SMALL-TALK →T*I*P*!←

right here.

This comes from Dorothy Buckhanan Wilson of Alpha Kappa Alpha Sorority, Inc. (For more on Dorothy, please see her Theory of Grace on page 110.)

As the international president of one of the largest women's groups in the world, Dorothy talks to many, many, maaaaaany people, and her strategy was one of the best I've ever heard. Her questions could only be asked of *that person*, rather than a more general "How are you enjoying the weekend?" sort of question.

"I'll ask about their jewelry—there are so many stories with people's jewelry!—or their name and just give them an opportunity to talk about themselves," she said. "I'm always curious about people—how did you come to be in the sorority? How did you come to live in Portland? How did you come to be here this weekend?"

Plus, she said, a small amount of observation goes a long way. "Oh, I noticed you're traveling with So-and-so; how did you two decide to travel together? I noticed you came on the train; why the train?"

Offer to set the pie on the counter or scan the room for the gift pile—anything that gets the object to its correct destination without blowing the host off-course.

"We brought y'all some flowers, and here's the canned clams you asked for—should we add them to that pyramid of clams over there?"

🍍 If you bring flowers, please bring them in a form that is ready to sit down on a surface, which is to say, in a vase. A wrapped bouquet is lovely *but* also requires someone to find a vase, turn on the faucet, cut the stems under the running water to the right height, then return to hosting duties. So, yeah, vase.

Now begins the Unspoken Norms Sleuthing portion of your evening! As a UNS detective, your first mystery will likely be the Mystery of Whether or Not to Take Off Your Shoes.🍍

If there are benches with rows of shoes under them, or you find yourself gazing upon an abundant field of what are clearly the other guests' shoes, then yes, take them off. If your host is not wearing outdoor shoes, offer. Most people *don't* wander around barefooted or in slippers unless they wish to broadcast something.

Other Important UNS Mysteries:

🌸 Where is the bathroom? (Use your feet and eyes!)

🌸 What level of saltiness, crudity, and profanity is appropriate in this setting? (Use your ears and your common sense!)

🌸 What are we eating? (This is not something you can ask unless you're 7 years old. You may, however, state that it smells *wonderful* in here, which will probably lead to a discussion of what, exactly, is creating that smell.)

🌸 When are we eating dinner? (You will know this when your host says something like "Why doesn't everyone take a seat/grab a plate/find the nearest cabana . . . ")

🌸 How formal is this dinner? Which fork is used when? (ALWAYS LOOK AT YOUR HOST! Truly. Don't eat until your host is eating unless they say otherwise; perhaps don't even sit until your host is seated, unless everyone else is seated and doing so would make them feel uncomfortable.)

🌸 When is it time to go? (Watch for "please get out" signs, mentioned earlier in the chapter.)

🍍 As a person who experiences and produces foot smells, I always hope it's a shoes-on house, but I've gotten burned enough times that now, if I don't *absolutely know* that I can keep my shoes on, well, foot preparation is *definitely* on the ahead-of-time list.

Cocktail hour! This is a wonderful time to get to chat with any guests you may not know well, *especially* if you know lots of people there and they don't. Ask how they know the hosts, ask if they live in this neighborhood, and if so, how long have they been here, ask them about li'l Trevin, Boy Capitalist and Captain of Tomorrow, ask them *whatever*. If you can, steer the topic toward something they seem very familiar with—people always love explaining things they know well. This is why, despite its tacky connotations, asking people about their work can be *fascinating*. A point-blank "So what do you do?" is way too abrupt, but a "Do you work with Trevinka at that wonderful Tiny Sweaters for Penguins Who Are Cold Foundation?" 🍍 will more than likely lead to the answer you seek.

When speaking in a group, make sure that you are in a horseshoe shape rather than a tight circle, which isn't welcoming to other guests. Try not to have both hands full—keep your drink in your left hand and try to be near a surface where you can set down your little appetizer plate.

If there is a horseshoe conversation going on, and it's *not* a tense discussion that you have zero to contribute to, feel free to join! "Hello! May I join you?" is a perfect opening, followed by "I'm Kelly—I met Trevinka a few years ago during a knit-a-thon. We made hats for toucans, which was new for us! The toucans rejected the hats, but Trevinka and I have been the best of friends ever since."

In this way, you are not just offering your name, but a relevant biographical detail that people may or may not seize upon. Either way, you're establishing an introduction that goes beyond just a name, which can be difficult to build on.

Try to remember names. I like to ask people about the spelling, because then I can visualize the name in my head as if I were writing it—"So is that Carrie with a C or a K?" If you do forget someone's name later, you can always say, "I'm so sorry, but would you remind me of your name?" It's okay. They probably forgot yours, too.

🍍 BEST FOUNDATION (even better than the Red-Panda Therapy for Nervous Ladies Center of Excellence).

WHEN you SIMPLY MUST
bail
So sorry! Oh my gosh, I am so...

Sometimes, we *think* we are going to what we assume to be a 3- or 4-hour party, but *actually* it is a 14-course meal and as the clock hits midnight, you are barely halfway through the olives and pickles course.

In these cases, you *can* decide on your curfew, particularly if it's a weeknight, you have kids, whatever.

About an hour before you *thought* you'd be leaving—say, 10:00 p.m., when it is abundantly clear that things will not be in any way winding down by 11:00, you may begin to make faint murmurs. At this moment, you are dropping the slightest dust mote of a hint that, despite the hosts' European sensibilities, you *are* hoping to return home before 2:00 a.m.

This will come in the form of something you say to *another* guest, *not* loudly or pointedly *but* within earshot—"Oh, we're so boring now; we're pretty much in bed by 11:00, no matter what. So it's wonderful to be out!" This establishes the norm that you are having a wonderful time *but also* are a person who needs sleep in order to survive.

When hour three rolls around and there is still no sign of dinner, one *might* ask their significant other what time that morning flight is—4:00 a.m? And, thus, the bailing-out trajectory has begun!

Here, the truth is "Had I known that I was signing up for an all-night party, I may have told the sitter that, or, more likely, just not come." Another truth at play here that your host is sliiiiightly bending the social contract.

Once you have a quiet, one-on-one moment with your host, assume a look that conveys deep sorrow, frustration with your own human limitations, and not even a glimmer of annoyance.

"Trevinka, I hate to say it, but I'm afraid that if my squadron of pugs doesn't get their dinner by 1:00 a.m. they *all* throw up in protest! On the white sofa! I'm so terribly sorry but I'm going to have to depart around 12:30. I so wish I could stay; Trevin is such a wonderful boy and so lucky to have you as his mother."

Ah, dinnertime! Perhaps it's a grab-your-plate-and-head-through-the-buffet event, in which case the only thing to keep in mind is mentally dividing the delicious dish by number of people present and making sure that you are taking at least 15 percent less than what seems like your fair share. This self-will can be very, very tricky when crab or shrimp are around, but not to worry: Either some foolish person at the table will be allergic to shellfish, or should worse come to worse, you can eat it another time.

If it is a seated dinner, then whoever brings you the dish gets some noises of delight and appreciation—this is *beautiful!*

Seating! It's a tricky one. If there are no place cards, then I normally consider how I rank in the order of guests. Not that any guest is more important than any other guest, buuuut . . . if this party is *for* someone, if there is a beloved family member or friend who lives far away and rarely gets time with everyone, if there is an elder or dignitary present, consider taking a seat toward either end of the table so that they may have the prime, central seats.

If there is someone at the party that you absolutely *adore* and never, ever get to see, well, a discreet whisper ahead of time—"Elisabeth! Can we sit together at dinner?"—is perfectly acceptable dinner-party strategy, but know that any number of things may pull that plan apart.

There is no need to sit right next to your significant other. Y'all get to sit next to each other enough.

This food is *wonderful*, and if you feel comfortable discussing food, you can and should point out things you find truly amazing. How did they learn to cook paella? Oh, the *sculpted marzipan!* This lime-cucumber-teriyaki agua fresca is a *revelation*—how did they get the brilliant idea to add beef jerky as a garnish?

Serving other people food you made is a vulnerable moment. You have put a lot into it; you are truly and fervently hoping people love it. My mother and I are absolutely famous for soliciting compliments on our cooking—if a good 15 minutes have gone by

There are very few nondignitary elders.

and no one has mentioned the appetizers for the fourth time, we might subtly steer the subject back to the Very Important Question of Whether We Did Good. Not gracious, but (hopefully) understandable.

So dole out those compliments and do not be shy. Notice the small things the host has done and love them. Any time they are going above and beyond what is the most basic act of giving nourishment to you (think place settings, decorations, complicated recipes, courses that go together, whatever it might be that is not just handing you a bowl of gruel à la *Oliver Twist*), *speak up and acknowledge them.*

You're eating slowly, putting your fork down between bites. If the conversation is one that you know you will want to weigh in on, forsake giant bites of bread. If you can't or won't stop with enormous bread bites, at least don't do that thing where you gesture that you have a point to make but your mouth is full and all conversation needs to stop for 25 seconds while you masticate. Likewise, if you want to ask someone a question, just watch them for, say, 3 seconds and make sure they are not about to put the perfectly composed bite of hummus, pita, and olive-with-pit in their mouth.

When is it time to go? Ah, this is such a complicated truth to discern. Following dinner, there *may* be an invitation to go through to the salon to enjoy a recorder concerto from Trevin. Or dessert may be the end. If there is no announcement of Exciting Immediate Future Events, then linger over your empty dessert plate just a bit. Your host does not want you to stay forever, and they will likely feel relieved when you announce that everything was *so* good, just delicious and beautiful and everything anyone would ever hope for in a party, and Trevin truly is the luckiest *and* most talented, bright, and driven boy ever to

"Above all things, avoid letting her know that you have found or felt insects in your bed, a circumstance that may chance sometimes to happen even in the best kept houses."

—Miss Leslie gives voice to our darkest fears.

> "Hospitality takes a high rank among the social virtues;
> but we fear it is not held in so high esteem as formerly.
> Its duties are often fatiguing and irksome, no doubt, and
> sometimes quite unnecessarily so."

—The *PMRE* needs you to relax; hosting is not that big a deal.

matriculate from the Wild Lily Child Full Potential Development Academy Community and Juggling Conservatory, and what a wonderful night this was.

Was. See that? Past tense, and everyone is okay with that. If this is a totally legitimate leaving time and you are not the first to leave the party, you should wish everyone a good night and say it was lovely to meet them or that you hope to see them again, thank your hosts, gather your things, and whisk away into the night.

If you are leaving a little *earlier* than other guests, please do not bring all conversation and happenings to a halt so that everyone may hail you farewell. A whisper to your host, a slight rustling, and then—"Oh, no, please continue! We must run but it has been so wonderful to see everyone!" is just right.

Get in the car, give yourself a high five, and drive away into the night, free as a bird. Smile with your whole face, entire body— perhaps your very soul, serene in the knowledge that you are moving ever closer to your couch, your cheese, your Netflix.

WHEN YOU are a houseguest

Houseguesting! The Final Frontier! Well, actually I suppose not in any way I can quantify or stand by, but it certainly is *something wonderful* for someone to love you so much that they want you to (temporarily) *live* with them, morning, noon, and night!

Here is the crux of the houseguest arrangement: Your host is going to do everything *they see fit* to make your stay comfortable and welcoming; in return, you are going to *joyfully accept without judgment whatever those accommodations may be.*

Let's do a run-through, shall we?

Before the house-guestin'

Yay! You've been invited to stay with someone! Usually, this is not quite as clear an offer as, say, "Would you like to come over for dinner at 7:00 p.m. next Friday?" but instead is a "Please come visit me in Metropolis!" offered weeks or months ago. This *may*, in fact, mean "please come visit me in Metropolis" or it *may* mean "I have enjoyed spending time with you, I like you, this is the end of our time together, so I will make these noises with my mouth because I feel like I should." It's a fun mystery!

Unless I have a well-established houseguesting relationship (or am related by blood or by many decades of excellent friendship), I do not like to ask directly. Normally, I will e-mail or text the people I want to see, let them know when I will be in town, and say that I would absolutely love to see them, perhaps adding "as much as possible!" to the end if that is true.

They may offer! That would be fantastic! They may not offer, in which case, probably don't ask! That is a big ask, and people feel uncomfortable saying no, so you're either making them say no to you or say yes, then feel a little bit resentful for you intruding on their space, timing, schedules, personal happenings, in-progress-but-not-announced gender transitions, whatever.

It's a date! Huzzah! Hattiesburg, Mississippi, here you come! Now, sort out the details—do you want to spend a *lot* of time with your host ("I'd love to spend every second you have free with you, but I *know* you are really busy finalizing that PhD thesis, so . . . ") or are you mostly occupied during your time there? ("I am *so excited to see you!* Because of the convention, I'm going to be out of your hair all day Friday, Saturday, and Sunday, but can we plan

(continued on page 180)

A FEW TIPS for when those wedding bells are a-ringin'!

Wedding Guest Dos

If you are a guest, congratulations! Your job is spectacularly simple.

- Send that RSVP in at the earliest possible second (verbal RSVPs *do not and will never count*).

- Purchase a gift in your price range, either from the registry or from your heart, then have it sent to whatever the return address is on the invitation, unless you are told otherwise. Bringing a gift to the wedding itself introduces several logistical challenges (Where does gift go? Who shall watch the gifts? Who shall transport the gifts?) in a day that is made of nothing but logistical challenges.

- Show up to the wedding at the time specified and in proper attire. If you're confused, feel free to ask a member of the wedding party or a family member what they're wearing. When in doubt, go one step more formal than you'd think. Stay away from dresses made of feathers and similarly attention-grabbing garb, plunging necklines, white and ivory, tie-dye, etc., etc.

- Be silent, respectful, and appropriately moved (or at least adopt the corresponding facial expression) during the ceremony, then enjoy the free booze, food, and general bonhomie.

- Feel free to compliment anyone who had a hand in the day, but be mindful of the fact that the bride and groom have no idea what is happening and are both probably overwhelmed, exhausted, and/or drunk. Plus, they are in a room with almost everyone in the world who is dear to them so if you see them regularly, cede the time to out-of-town guests.

One of my favorite memories is Alan Kaplan, who is a second dad to me, cheerfully telling me that he had more fun at my wedding than his own.

Wedding Guest Don'ts

If you are a guest, under no circumstances may you do the following:

- Call or text the bride with questions about the event within a month of the wedding. *Please do not do this.* As my darling mentor Nancy Kaffer puts it, being a bride is like being the CEO of a small, motivated, yet terribly incompetent company. I'd go one step further and add that in this scenario, the company does not yet have access to any sort of communication strategies or technology other than the CEO Bride herself, who is assumed to be both omnipotent and, for some reason, relaxed enough to be cheerfully in the center of a 124-person game of Telephone. *Unless you are calling her to inform her that the kidney she has been waiting for has arrived, call someone else.* Or, better yet, don't!︎

- Take photos of the ceremony unless you are being paid to do so. Just be present. This moment will be properly documented.

- Enjoy so many of the signature cocktail︎︎ that you find yourself moved to give a toast that neither you nor anyone else had planned on or asked for.

- Say you can't make it then, miraculously, the day of show up, a real-life Eris hurtling an Apple of Seating Chart Discord.

- Wear your *own* wedding gown in the spirit of solidarity and sisterhood.

(continued)

︎ The answers to nearly every question you might have already exist in the world, most likely on the wedding Web site.

︎︎ Ugh. But fine.

a little advice FOR BRIDES OR GROOMS
who are MOSTLY in charge of planning & execution

Poor brides and grooms! So alone! No one to give them unsolicited advice! No one airing strongly held and *surprising* opinions about how the day should go! No Matrimonial Industrial Complex to tell them that unless they do X, Y, and Z to 837 mason jars, their love isn't real and are they *even actually getting married?*

Just kidding! I was a bride once! In fact, I'd go so far as to call myself a fairly successful bride🍍 insofar as I planned and pulled off a wedding that cost an amount that seemed reasonable and everyone had gobs of fun. Here's how I did it:

1. **Decided ahead of time not to look at Pinterest:** I stuck to this until 2 weeks before the ceremony, when I *did* look at it. Waves of acid regret slammed into me and left regret burns all over; my wedding wasn't going to contain things that I had never even considered before looking at Pinterest and yet now seemed utterly vital in the same way a groom is vital. *I was about to throw a travesty of a wedding!* Then I got back off Pinterest and felt loads better.

2. **Established my four wedding priorities:**

    * *Get married.*

    * *Look beautiful in my wedding dress.*

    * *Have a wedding where everyone has that happy, joyful feeling and gets drunk and dances and meets new people.*

    * *Not make anyone's life, including mine, a nightmare in the process.*

🍍 Unfortunately, less so in the "being married" department, though that is a story for another time, by which I mean never.

Once said priorities were in place, whenever making a decision that would cost time, money, or energy, I could ask whether it supported those goals. If it didn't, I didn't need to bother. There were so, so many things to bother with already.

3. **Put special care and love into things that had people's names on them,** namely, the invitations and wedding favor boxes. I wanted everyone to know how much their presence meant.

4. **Invited significant others but not plus-ones:** Single guests were quietly apprised of the other single people there whom they might find interesting and could go ahead and look up on Facebook. And then, there were lots of fun wedding-night hookups that I would *not* have called ahead of time but were, in retrospect, just right. I also made sure that anyone who was coming solo knew at least three people at the wedding well; had someone not been connected, of course, I would want them to have a familiar face by their side.

5. **Made peace with the fact that many things would not go precisely the way I wanted them to** but, barring an *actual emergency*, things would be fine. And then they were!

a little advice FOR BRIDES OR GROOMS who are NOT shouldering primary effort in planning

If you can't be helpful, *then at least have the good sense not to hinder.* Just agree with everything your spouse-to-be says, even if it directly contradicts something he or she said 15 seconds prior. If his or her behavior is *truly* appalling and unprecedented and they do not respond to gentle suggestions, well, there's still time to reconsider whether you wish to bind yourself legally and emotionally to this person.

to hang out on one or more of the evenings?")

Is your significant other, your best friend, or your emotional-support ferret coming? If so, y'know, don't assume the invitation extends to them, but check. ("I'm dying to stay with you, but would it be too much for you to have me *and* Eleanor?")

Also, be *very, very* crystal-transparent-perhaps-there-aren't-even-molecules-here clear about when you are arriving and when you are departing. Then, so far as it is within your power, arrive and depart *at those times*.

If your host offers to pick you up at the airport/train station/stagecoach depot, that's great, and you can and should accept, perhaps offering a small "Gosh, are you sure?" for confirmation.

However, if you are arriving at a late or inconvenient hour, pre-empt with "You know, I'm getting in at 3:37 a.m. and planning on cabbing it to your house—is there a good way to get inside without waking you up?" If they insist, push back once more, and then, the third offer you may accept if it is given in a hearty, sincere tone.

Now to get a thoughtful present (perhaps more than one, if you are visiting roommates or a family!), pack those bags, annnnd . . .

BE THE *Best* HOUSE guest

As you probably noticed from that section on *having* houseguests, it's tough! There are some people to whom long-term hosting comes very naturally and a houseguest doesn't bother them a *bit*. They are *more than happy to have you stay forever* because this is *fun!* Here I will note that there are also humans who can run the 100-yard dash in under 10 seconds and others who command vast armadas to fulfill their military and/or personal aims on the high sea. So let's go ahead and assume you are staying with someone more within the normal bell curve of houseguest emotions.

What they will do to make your stay comfortable (physically, emotionally, spiritually, and yes, perhaps even sexually! 🍍) is

🍍 For more on this, see When You are Hosting . . . a *Lover!* on page 158.

entirely their decision. You may take *note* of these things and verbalize delight. You may *also* quietly ask yourself if, given the opportunity to do it again, you would *want* to sleep on a depressed blow-up mattress while never even *mentioning* gluten (the word itself is a trigger) while an enormous fleet of elderly terriers patrol vigilantly. That answer may in fact be, "That was *quite* the time; I learned *a lot*. I learned about myself; I learned about congenital terrier-eye issues. And I never, ever need to do that again." 🍍

You may not, however, under any circumstances, convey any emotion less positive than awestruck joy at their generosity and your accommodations. 🍍🍍

Your task, meanwhile, is to *have as light a footprint as possible*. Here, you should channel a very friendly ghostliness: You appear at appropriate times, bringing joy, good humor, and gifts with you. 🍍🍍🍍

Aside from those times, your hosts should never be overly aware of your presence through sights, sounds, or (deep sigh about my feet) *smells*.

It's appropriate, when you arrive, if the answers aren't given or apparent, to ask the following questions:

🍍 What is the WiFi password? 🍍🍍🍍🍍

🍍 Where is a good place to shower?

🍍 And, should your host invite you again, you may have developed some breed-specific allergy that only crops up at night but you want to spend *every single moment* with them during the daytime, then flee to the hotel each night.

🍍🍍 You must *never* express these thoughts to the general public. A brief complaining outburst to your best friend or S.O.? Sure! Describe those beady, crusty little eyes in great detail and be done with it. But this may never become an anecdote you tell. Someone let you into their home and trusted you with their privacy. Respect that.

🍍🍍🍍 Actually I'm not sure ghosts are like that, even friendly ones. Maybe we'll go with fairy godmother-esque.

🍍🍍🍍🍍 I'm sorry to say that this question is almost always my top priority.

- May I store groceries in the fridge?

- Is there anything I should know about the apartment or the room?

- Are there any Very Special Things that can't be replaced with money in here? (Don't say it that way, but if something looks antique or expensive, ask about it.)

- In terms of coming and going, is there anything I should know about locking and unlocking?

- When can I take every single person hosting me out to a *very* nice dinner or, if that is beyond my means, when can I cook y'all dinner? (Again, don't say exactly that—just ask if there's a night you can take them out.)

- And so on . . .

It's always nice to ask your host for recommendations of what to do, see, and taste in their town, and this *also* offers *them* the chance to join you. It is good to be as self-reliant as one can be. Under no circumstances may you bound downstairs in the morning with the "HELLO! GOOD MORNING!!!! What are we gonna DO today? Is today the day we go to the pool? Are we gonna do archery? Will you be my hiking buddy?" or anything else that an excitable 8-year-old camper might ask of his counselor.

One time—this is a true story—I was staying with someone, and she had a perfectly lovely but also fairly ordinary (to my unrefined eyes) bowl sitting by the bedside. At one point, I washed it out and then put some yogurt in it and then washed it out again. The next time I saw her in the kitchen, her eyes flashed to the bowl, then to me, at which point I was informed that—just for my own information! for future reference!—that is actually a 200-year-old bowl by a renowned and definitely deceased potter and is pretty much irreplaceable, but if it *were* replaceable, it would not cost what I assume a nice bowl would cost ($10? $20? I thought it was Fiestaware!) but a very large amount. This prompted me to ask what other priceless treasures were in the room, and there were a *lot,* and I was *really glad I knew that.*

Also verboten: waking them up in the middle of the night to accompany you to the outhouse because that campfire story scared you *or* wetting the bed in lieu of going to the outhouse alone. Yes, 1999 Tumalo yurt at Cascade Science School, I am looking *squarely* at y'all.

"Allow their presence to interfere as little as possible with your domestic arrangements; thus letting them see that their visit does not disturb you, but that they fall, as it were, naturally into a vacant place in your household."

<hr/>

—Oh man, I so wish I could be as cool a host as Samuel Wells.

Please do remember that for you, this is a fun vacation (adult camp!), but for your host, this is their real life with all the real-life things you have to do when you're not on vacation. Hopefully *they* will switch their schedule up because they want to sip every drop out of the honeysuckle blossom of your presence, but . . . maybe they can't. Maybe, even, they don't want to. So please, do not in any instance look upon them as your own personal, free tour guide.

It's also nice to keep the room you're in as tidy as possible even if, like me, your room at home often contains haystacks of clothing. I like for the room always to be in a state where I can happily leave the door open, therefore announcing my presence or lack thereof to the host.

There you go! Off to the races! You're a staaaaaaaar of being tidy, *not* eating people's prosciutto until they expressly invite you to do so, not making a ton of noise at night, not rifling through drawers and bathroom cupboards, and so on!

A BRIEF *Conclusion*

Go forth, darlings, go visit and eat and entertain and scrape every bit of the marrow that is friendship. Go boldly, inviting people into *your* habitat and, perhaps, being invited into *theirs*.

And never forget: The better a guest you are, the more likely it is that people will not only consent, but instead will ask—*beg!*—for your presence.

As an aside, one time I met a precious young lady named Elsa in Italy who was the daughter of a family friend. We were chatting with her and telling her to come visit us in Oregon the next time she was in the United States,⚜ and then she said *what I had been waiting my entire life to hear.*

"Oh! So! You know, my fahzer, he has a beeg, beeg, BEEG boat! And next time you are een Sicily, during the summer, just come get on the *boat*! Beecause we are alvays sailing during ze summer! Oh! We go EVERYWHERE—Sardeeeenia, the Capriiiiiis, Corsicaaaaaah, Majorca! You just come! Come get on the boat! We'll go everywhere! You can have your own cabeen!"

I have yet to take Elsa up on her offer, because first I need to show her the *best time ever* in Oregon.

But someday, I *will* get on that beeg, beeg, BEEG boat. In fact, let us all get on that (proverbial) beeg boat, and sail away, companionable hosts and gracious guests all.

⚜ Elsa does a *lot* of traveling, as the punch line of this anecdote will make clear.

CHAPTER SEVEN

LET'S MAKE THIS DAY

Gracious as Heck!

ood morning! You're alive! This is, in and of itself, some *spectacular* news, and I for one am glad to hear it.

Please, go ahead and take a moment. Stretch and blink sleepily. If you are, like me, a dream babbler, finish that fascinating play-by-play; 🍍 pet the cat who is sitting on your chest and has been waiting for this moment; say good morning to whatever sentient being you may be waking up next to, because they deserve it even if they were misbehaving the night before and/or is not someone you particularly want to see as soon as you open your eyes.

Now, smile big and slingshot your eye mask toward the ceiling in a festive, celebratory manner. Because you know what? Today is going to be *one g-d gracious day!*

Let us journey together, as you do your very best, avoiding all manner of traps, snares, and bedevilments, floating through à la Aphrodite on a clamshell. A *nice* clamshell. Your little cherubs are there, too, and when they are not busy tending to your beautiful, flowing locks, they are encouraging you to be the *best*

🍍 "So then *you* were there but you were *actually* Christina Hendricks but *I* knew it was you, and you-as-Christina told me that the Math for Moms party would be starting soon so I'd better make sure that my abacus was polished, which worried *me*, because I knew I needed my *abacus,* but every time I tried to polish mine it kept turning into a *dormouse,* but . . ."

you, and who can say no to tiny, naked, flying, articulate babies? Not you, gracious lady or gracious man or gracious nonbinary person!

As those cherubs hover nearby, there are important questions in the air. One, how did cherubs become a thing and how are they still a thing? It's odd, right? But two, and more saliently, *who do you want to be today?*

That question is a bit more complicated than what's on your to-do list or a nagging feeling about a Pilates class that you wish you wanted to go to. It's more than needing to be at X place at Y time, though all those details should be examined.

But really, the question is who do *you* want to *be* today? Neither I nor the cherubs can answer that, but here are some things I like to decide on.

- Today, I *want* to pause before I react to things.

- Today, no matter how anyone else behaves, I want to be good and decent.

- Today, I want to be productive and do the work that needs doing, which means that today is not a day when I can have long, in-depth conversations with every human and friendly dog I come across, but I can politely excuse myself or explain that I am on a tight deadline and would love to catch up soon.

- Today, I am feeling sad, so I want to be extra kind to those around me, because maybe they're sad, too, and being kind even when I don't feel like it normally cheers me up.

"Make it a rule to repeat to your friends all the pleasant remarks that (as far as you know) are made on them, and you will increase their happiness, and your own popularity."

—Miss Leslie is the most positive Machiavellian ever.

Perfect! Now you know what you want to do—or, as the former yoga teacher in me would say, you have *set your loving intention.*🍍

It's so easy to be gracious in bed, isn't it? But now we must face the day, even though it is too bright and probably way colder and less pleasant than our bed. Perhaps you can ease this transition, as I do, by having a soft, fleecy rug right beside your bed? And hanging above it, that robe that feels like God giving you a very warm hug? And slippers? Whatever does it for you, preparing a little transition between bed and the rest of the world can start the morning on a much better footing than when you have to stumble around on a cold floor hoping that there's a towel down there clean enough to use after your shower.

Now, as you get ready, I would ask something of you. It's not a small thing, but hopefully you will hear this as I mean it and not as a bunch of giant interlocking industries that intentionally make women feel bad about themselves mean it.

If you have it in you, put yourself together carefully. Do your face. Grab something you want to wear. Look *nice.*🍍🍍

Nice does not mean wearing painful high heels, or spending hours on your makeup, or making sure that no follicle besides those

(continued on page 191)

🍍 To be fair, I was a yoga teacher for about 10 minutes at a small-town YMCA, and most of my fellow yogis were in their late seventies, and the only reason I was a yoga teacher was that they needed a substitute and I had attended enough of my friend April's classes that I could do a pretty good impression. Every now and again, I would sneak something deeply weird in: "Now, as you slowly, one vertebra at a time, roll that spine down, I'd like you to imagine your own spine. Just visualize it, for a minute, as you roll slowly, slowly down. Breathe in, breathe out, think your spine thoughts annnnnnd relax. Inhale, hug your knees to your chest, gently rolling to massage your back. Exhale, remembering that everyone you love has a skeleton inside them at all times."

🍍🍍 Exempted from this: mothers who would cut off their own pinkie for enough time to poop in peace, let alone spend mental energy on themselves, and everyone else who is similarly time/energy-strapped. The pleasure and privilege of getting ready is to be enjoyed, and if you can't enjoy it, then of course don't worry about it! You don't need to create a fine appearance for anyone but yourself, and if your priorities are elsewhere, then that's just that!

A FEW *Stylish Thoughts...*

- There is absolutely nothing wrong with wearing something similar every day. Almost everything in my wardrobe is navy, white, gold, or cognac-colored leather. Therefore, everything matches everything else! If someone wants to tell me my life color scheme is silly, that is a them-problem. I'll be over here, never wasting a minute wondering if I match or not.

- Jewelry! Maybe you hate it! If so, go ahead and skip this part. I am a big, big, big fan of pearls, because I think they go with everything and make everything look nicer and they come from the ocean and I could go on and on. But maybe you love silver. Or gold. Or peridot or leather or a narwhal's tusk or *whatever*. Don't feel bad for a second about wearing the same jewelry every day. Also, a big investment in a necklace/bracelet/whatever for yourself can absolutely be worth it and, if you have the money, doesn't need to be justified to anyone. Will it last forever? Will you want to wear it every day? Will it bring you joy every day that you wear it? If the answer to those questions is yes, make the splurge happily. It can be your thing, and when you are about to die, you can pick someone who will love it as much as you love it and it can be their thing.

- Quality over quantity. I have two pairs of boots that are 15+ years old. One was a hand-me-down from my godmother, and another is a pair of Ferragamo boots from the '90s I got on eBay for $40. I treat them well (leather conditioner! always, always, leather conditioner!), and they look classic and beautiful and will never go out of style.

- Other items that it's worth spending some money on: classic black pumps (or brown or navy or your dark color of choice), a very warm winter coat, a stylish spring and fall coat, and a sturdy-ass handbag that your laptop can fit into.

- When you hit the thrift store (or, I guess, the regular store, though I find older clothing to be better made, more flattering, and generally more interesting and less likely to look dated quickly), shop in sizes larger than yours and get it tailored. A beautiful $15 dress deserves a $25 tailor because when it fits you perfectly, it will look like a $200 dress.

- I swear this is the last thing I will say about cognac-colored leather, but seriously, it's the best. It goes beautifully with black, darker brown, navy, whites, neutrals, and even jewel tones and pastels. It gets along so well with *everyone* and I adore it. Camel-colored coat + cognac boots + cognac handbag = wear anything in the world with it and it'll look right.

- Finally—this is from a Bobbi Brown makeup book, and I can't remember which one—but there was a "Is it time to change up your makeup routine?" quiz, and one of the questions was "Do you wear red lipstick every day?" This was coming after a lot of similar questions that *clearly* were leading to the "Girl, you're in a style rut! Shake it up, girlfriend!" answer, BUT! Bobbi blew me away. She said something to the effect of, "If you wear red lipstick every day, don't you dare stop." I'm a redhead with piglet coloring and by all logic and reason, I should *not* wear red lipstick. But it makes me happy, so I do wear it. Every. Day. You can pry my 24-hour matte red lipstick from my cold, dead hands.

(continued)

A Few Stylish Thoughts (*cont.*)

🐚 There may be some style thing that you think, Huh—I would *love* to be able to do that, but when I try to do my hair, it's like my fingers are made of ham. Even though I want to give up, me and my ham fingers persevere. If I keep trying it, eventually I will get it down because it's not rocket science, it's hair attached to my head and eventually it's going to kind of do what I want it to and that's a nice compromise.

🐚 My New Year's resolution tends to be style-based (because accomplishing it will be fun and not the normal resolution letdown that no, I have *not* magically become a different person as the clock strikes midnight; can I change; can *anyone* really change, why is life as it is? Etc., forever). In 2010, I decided that by God, *I wanted to be able to give myself a rad beehive*. January, February—these were tough months, with floppy bouffants that fell like so many disappointing soufflés. But! By July, I had it *nailed*. And now I can always give myself a beehive! Almost everything in the world, and *certainly* any hairdo, can be mastered with practice and patience.

🐚 If you, like me, are a red lipstick lady, or even just a bright color lady, I have a few tips. Go to Sephora or Ulta and try on every single red lipstick (or magenta lip gloss or yellow eye shadow) until you find the right one. Apply whatever it is carefully—if it's on your lips, line and fill them first, then apply with a brush; if it's an eye shadow or blush, put on a primer and set it afterward with translucent powder. Push it to the limit, my friend, and never, ever apologize for being fancy.

on your head shows any shred of existence. Nice doesn't mean expensive clothing; nice doesn't mean cruel shape-wear garments intended to disguise the fact that you have a human body.

Nice is not an arbitrary standard of What Humans Should Look Like. Nice is what makes *you* feel powerful and strong and like the things on your body are not accidents, but purposeful choices.

Nice is the dress or pants that are perfect and why didn't you buy this in every color? Nice is the jewelry that reminds you of something wonderful, nice is the lipstick that you splurged on because it's just perfect. Nice is whatever it is that *makes you feel like the best version of yourself.*

Once, in Mississippi, I was doing a story on hat culture 🍍 and the amazing women who wear hats every day. I mostly pitched this to have an excuse to talk to these lionesses, because they invariably looked *flawless.* Not because they were rich. Not because they had nothing to do with their time besides primp. Because they had made the decision to reflect something inside outward, in hat form, to the delight of the community (me).

I asked one woman, Why so many hats? Why wear a hat every day?

"Welllllll," she drawled, then paused. "You know, Kelly, here's how Ahhhhh see it. Ah could be hit by a bus—tomorrow! And if, Gahd *forbid,* I get hit by a bus tomorrow, I should wear this fabulous hat today."

The connection between hats and morbidity makes perfect sense to me, but may not resonate. If not, here is what she was saying. Fully and joyfully executing her best life meant wearing things that she loves and not letting a day go by where she hasn't done everything she can to make herself feel good. She brings people, *most of all herself,* joy with her hats.

So whatever it is that makes you feel like that—wear it. Take

🍍 Of or pertaining to the wearing of fanciful hats, as a lifestyle. I for one encourage anyone reading this to start a *Hat Culture* magazine. *Hat Fancy*? I'd subscribe, and I'll bet you would, too.

care of it. Walk out the door knowing that if that Sudden-Death Rhetorical Device Bus were to mow you down, you would have zero regret in your style. Wear your (proverbial) fabulous hat today.

Remember, lovelies, that clothes are things we put on ourselves to prevent hypothermia and be in compliance with nudity law, but they are also a great opportunity to make the world look a tiny bit more like we wish it would look.

Style is not about money. It's not about slavishly following fashion magazines. It is how you present yourself to the world. It is how you choose to do your hair, even if it's a ballerina bun every day. If it brings you joy and energy, then wear it.

Furthermore, if it brings you joy, treat it kindly. If it wants to be hung up, hang it up. If some mud gets on your shoes, wipe it off before it stains.

Perhaps you've already laid out your outfit the night before. Wonderful! If not, then check the weather and go with your heart.

Of course, there is nothing in the world forcing you to spend time getting ready, and you certainly shouldn't do it because you feel pressured to, or because there are vast industries out there that make money by making *you* feel bad about your body, or #Patriarchy. Wear the clothes that you love, put everything or nothing on your face, slide on the accessories that make you happy when you look at them, whether that's Great-Grandmother Ophelia Vanderbilt's opera pearls or a happy cuttlefish-playing-Xbox necklace.

Here, again, I think it's the difference between a stranger telling you to smile versus making the decision to pay attention to the good and, as a matter of consequence, smiling more. Pause and think—what shall I do with this damn hair? Is this a red-lipstick

ALWAYS the Patriarchy. Every time.

Etsy!

day or a barefaced morning? Whatever that plan is, execute it with as much precision *and* happiness as you can. I think of putting on my makeup as a chance to do some art on my own face.

You look *marvelous*. Off into the world we go!

A BRIEF NOTE BEFORE *we begin*...

Please remember that safety always, always, ALWAYS trumps politeness. If you ever have a funny feeling about a situation, it's okay to listen—it's your lizard brain talking! In your lizard brain is stored the collective sense of infinite generations of people (. . . apes, mammals, amoeba . . .) who were *not* eaten by alligators or fellow one-celled organisms. So when and if a person, place, or situation makes you uneasy or afraid, listen to that feeling and do what's necessary to extricate yourself. *Gracious to yourself, y'all.*

A SLIGHTLY LESS-BRIEF NOTE

You may read the following and think, WOW. She has *really gone for it* in explaining how to ride the subway. What is this—three pages? On how to get on the metro?

And yes, yes, I did, for a good reason, l'il pelican, and not just because I am writing this upon returning from New York, where I finally conquered my fears!

Using a subway is the purest distillation of an ungracious public situation. All elements are covered—waiting in lines, walking in a packed crowd, getting into and out of a tight, shared space, moving through a sea of indifferent humanity, smelling others, enduring frightening behavior, and finding ways we can stay comfortable without disturbing others.

Because of this, that one experience stands in for an entire host of other situations, including but not limited to grocery shopping! Riding an elevator! Going through airport security! Walking down a crowded city street! And so on. Follow these rules and you will be able to navigate any public situation.

Mass Transit Principles

I approach mass transit (and any crowded situation that I find myself in) with two goals:

1. To shed the ego of self, becoming one with the flowing river of humanity, which means definitely *not* standing on the side of the escalator that people are trying to walk down.

2. To pass the time in a safe yet comfortable manner until I can not be enclosed in a small metal container, neck deep in humanity, some of whom may do things that may run counter to that "safe yet comfortable" bit.

Before you enter this, it's worth taking a few moments to peer into the immediate future and *plan* for it, so that you may artfully dance through this train station: How shall you pay for this trip? Is that payment in your hand? Is there any immediate need physically, like arranging your stuff? Do you look like one of my Irish forebears as they disembark after a long, rough sea voyage, clasping in your arms your possessions, hopes, and dreams, plus two energy drinks? If so, sort out that situation *before* you are on the escalator.

Do the same in airport security lines, the checkout at 7-Eleven, etc. Be prepared, as the Boy Scouts would say, so that you are not the person who falls over in her haste to take off her boots as the other passengers eye her angrily.

Go with the flow! If you are in the herd, move with the herd. If you must pause en route to the train/subway/etc., carefully maneuver yourself out of the flow first. Nestling behind the MetroCard machine is a perfect place to send that text/get that rock out of your shoe/put some space between you and someone who seems to be connecting with a reality that is not yours and shouting about it.

But—returning once more to questions of river hydraulics—there are places that are *not great* to stop, and those are the places where the pathway is narrower and therefore the water (or people) have to flow faster. Here, call upon your physical grace and be aware of the humans around you, how they are moving, where they are going, and, if possible, draft in their wake. In this way, the river flows and we all get to get off the subway, which is all I ever want.

Oh, ho! Sounds and smells tell you that your mass transit vessel is approaching! Stand back, for safety, and also because—this is a very basic physics principle that, sometimes, still escapes us—when people exit the small space, there is more room for you and others to *enter* the small space, so let them flow out before you flow in. You will get there. You will. And when you do, maybe this train car/bus/gondola is jam-packed with people. If so, there's very little you can do. Anchor yourself as best you can, make your footprint as small as possible, feel free to shoot dirty looks at anyone who violates your tiny bubble and doesn't apologize. If they *really* violate your bubble in intentional, predatory ways, feel free to *really* violate normal norms of volume.

Yelling "SIR? WHY DID YOU GRAB ME, SIR? ARE YOU GOING TO GRAB MY BUTT AGAIN? I WISH YOU WOULDN'T, SIR. IT'S VIOLATING AND I DON'T CARE FOR IT ONE BIT" is an extremely gracious, and helpful to others, reaction. Never underestimate the power of a well-deserved public shaming.

Maybe, if it's summertime and/or the humanity's ripe, breathe through your mouth or—this is something I actually do—put some sunscreen or lotion on your hands, then casually rest that hand on your face. A smell more powerful, and palatable, than what you were smelling!

Perhaps it's a lucky day, where the seats are ample, the train is quiet, and the podcast of choice is precisely the right length. Hurrah! Grab a seat and enjoy yourself, but not *too* much.

"We all have different levels of tolerance and comfort zones," Lizzie Post said. "The observed norm in the cabins is that the little space around you is your little space, and no one should be paying attention to it. People *aren't* going to be paying attention to you listening to a podcast, writing that report, or texting your friend, but they do end up paying attention if you clip your toenails or are dripping that breakfast burrito all over the floor."

As Lizzie pointed out, when you clip your toenails—*where do those toenails go?* Into the eensiest rip in the space-time continuum, never to be seen again?🍍 Or onto an innocent bystander's Kindle?🍍🍍

"When it comes to personal care, especially regarding hygiene, you save that to take to a restroom or private area," she said. "And that goes for conversations as well. The very personal details of medical life, not appropriate. The fact that you have a doctor's appointment, fine."

Lizzie also noted that cell phone conversations in public-yet-confined spaces really are just not great.

"People find it much harder to (tune out) when they can only hear half of the conversation," she said. "They find themselves trying to fill in the other half."

Seating always poses a question: Who, if anyone, in this car deserves this precious seat more than you? In lots of cases, the answer is no one! Yay! Savor that sweet-ass seat. However, anyone who looks as though they are in pain or especially tired (assuming you are neither of those things); anyone who is elderly and not in that vigorous just-got-back-from-speed-walking way; anyone who *clearly broadcasts they are pregnant (or would like others to think they are) by sporting a very round, protuberant belly that they*

🍍 No.

🍍🍍 Yes.

repeatedly pat in a proud, maternal manner—it is a good and noble thing to ask if they would like your seat.

When someone is in physical pain, life generally is tough. When you notice the people around you and see that need, acknowledging it in a way that doesn't call attention or broadcast pity is just about the best thing you can do.

Make eye contact, smile, ask—"Excuse me, would you like this seat?" By calling it "this" instead of "my," it takes you out of the equation and acknowledges that while you are currently occupying one, those seats belong equally to everyone in this public space.

Tragically, there are many, many people in the world—and I'm going to go out on a limb here and say that the majority are men— who feel free to take up more than their fair share of seating through spreading their knees as wide as possible, because . . . testicles? I don't know.

Anyhow, should you find this to be the case, you are more than free to, again, smile brightly and say, "Is this seat taken?" to the seat they are spreading over.

WHEN Someone ASKS FOR Money...

This was a thought from lovely Lelia Gowland, who in turn got it from one of her friends who advocates for and works with the homeless of New Orleans.

Lelia said a good principle is to treat someone who is asking others for money as you would someone who is working on commission. That is their job, in the same way that the guy at a cell phone store's job is to up-sell you on a fancy new phone. That is how they make money.

Just as you say, "No, thank you!" the fourteenth time you are given the chance to sign up for a Discount Store Credit Card, so you can kindly decline the opportunity to give someone money that you don't feel like. "Sorry!" and a smile is just fine.

GRACIOUS DRIVING

There is never a time when attention to those around you is even 1 percent as vital as when you are commanding a giant ball of metal moving at 70 miles per hour.

This is the very, very best moment to be present and focused, because, although cars are fantastic, driving represents the only time most of us could kill a bunch of people by being distracted for a few moments.

Fantastically enough, gracious driving *is* good driving, because you are always aware, you are willing to make small sacrifices in the service of the common good (everyone getting to where they're going safely and quickly), *and* it's a great challenge with little to no personal payoff, but great payoffs when we *all* do it.

- In general, the best policy is to go with the flow, keeping your attention moving constantly between what is happening ahead of you, what is happening behind you, and what you are doing.

- In very slow traffic, why not let that person trying to merge in merge in? It's the kind thing to do.

- One must never be a line cutter themselves; do not zip merrily along in the totally clear left lane then merge into the stop-and-go right lane at the last possible moment to make your turn.

I was trying to think of another example and I can't, short of sawmill employees—anyone in charge of giant spinning blades, really.

A Brief Note on Smiling

You'll notice that many, many of these small acts come with a suggestion to smile. In fact, when I was talking to these gracious people, almost *all* of them mentioned smiling and eye contact *immediately*. This caused an unpleasant frisson within me; I *hate* it when strangers

- Just like rude people, you can and should get away from rude drivers. If someone is driving erratically, try to get *ahead* of them, so that any shenanigans they may cause will be in your rearview mirror.

- I am a big advocate of the Pittsburgh left: For cars trying to make an unprotected left turn at an intersection, the first oncoming driver will let them turn first at the green light, thus making sure that no one has to endure the unendurable act of watching the light go from green to yellow to red, again and again, as their life slips away from them.

- If someone is singing and dancing in their car, pretend you don't see them, because that's a great joy we should all be able to indulge in when the mood strikes.

- If you see something wrong with someone's car (something falling off, a flat tire, etc.) then you may try to alert them at a stoplight. But not while they're driving. They won't understand, and in the meantime, you're not doing your best driving.

- If safety and personal comfort permit, it's always kind to stop and check on someone whose car is on the side of the road.

- When someone does something sweet for you on the road, roll down your window and give a thankful wave.

tell me to smile, thus suggesting that my face is not up to whatever lady-face standards they not only possess but also decided to voice to a stranger.

And yet, here I go, telling all y'all to smile when possible. It is important. It does make others and, more importantly, you happy.

It broadcasts that you are not upset or angry, which makes others way, way more receptive to whatever you're asking of them. It tells someone that you *see* them, that they exist, and this doesn't displease you. It is a small, universal, ancient action that really can change things.

"Be aware of the regard on your face; make a habit of it," Virginia Provosty said. "If you're centered and you know who you are and what you're doing in this world, you're not going to have a sour look on your face."

So if you don't want to smile, you don't have to. No need to go through life grinning like an idiot. But beginning any interaction with a smile, saying hello, asking someone how their day has gone thus far—well, just try it. Just do it for an afternoon. You'll see.

Traveling Farther Afield via Airplane

A brief show of hands: Whose favorite part of travel is the airport? Indeed. The experience of modern air travel is an unsettling time. One *must* arrive *on* time with *all* your belongings for the *sheer pleasure* of standing *very quietly* in a *very long* line. At the end of this line is not a *ferris wheel* ride or *ice cream*, but rather the *forced removal of your clothing,* the rush to get *this* item in *that* bin, and is it a *tablet* or a *laptop*? Then, assuming there is no need to search the bag and touch every item in there, you reassemble yourself and walk *miles* through soulless underground tunnels to *sit very quietly* and *very patiently* until it's time for you to be crammed like so much livestock into a *High-Velocity Death Can That Is Way, Way Too Cold.*

Rarely are you so subject to Fortuna's will. For it is *entirely not up to you* how this will go, whether everything is on time, how the weather is, whether you shall sit on the tarmac for 3 hours or end

Fine, just your shoes, and yet!

I for one advocate an immediate return to steamship travel.

up sleeping outside security, and (if you are lucky enough to get on the godforsaken contraption) whom you will be sitting next to, whether they will share your desire to pass the time as quickly and noninteractively as possible before a (Lord willing and the creek don't rise) safe return to land. Fun!

I have seen, in times of disaster that touches everyone, the fundamental goodness of humanity. You can also often witness this during the godforsaken *ordeal*—nay, *terrordrome*—that is domestic travel.

Here are a few ways to survive the unsurvivable.

- Dress up to fly! The key, here, is *long-sleeved jersey tunic or maxi jersey dress in a solid color*, perhaps with leggings and boots underneath. This outfit is as comfortable as pajamas without implying, as pajamas do, that the airport is your bedroom, your fellow travelers roommates or lovers who have earned the exquisite privilege of seeing you in nighttime garb. Plus, this combined with the below, is much more likely to get you bumped up to first class.

- We have talked about smiling and saying hello to people during commercial interactions. *This is never, ever so important as it is during air travel.* In certain situations where the stakes are actually high—say, at the hospital, advocating for a very sick family member—politeness is just not as important as conveying and receiving necessary information from the people who have a lot of control over the outcome. However, at the airport, the person working for the airline is *almost certainly blameless* for whatever is troubling passengers, yet they are *almost certainly going to bear the brunt of that anger.* I assure you, this JetBlue

Forward all my mail to the sea; I will send for my belongings presently.

SO UNCIVILIZED! Fine, I'm done. I promise I'm done.

Just kidding, I will never, ever cease speaking truth to power (read: complaining) about how wretched flying is.

representative is not a witch who conjured this seven-state-wide storm front for funsies. If she is and she did, then be *extra polite* because who wants a Storm Witch of that power and capacity mad at them? Not me. No sir. Not today. Not on this lovely Tuesday.

🐚 "Hello! How has your day been?" is the perfect greeting. If you *know* that this is a fraught time for airline employees (and really, when isn't it?), then a sympathetic smile and a "Hello! I can't *believe* this (weather/systematic delay/marauding band of hangar-size kittens that Storm Witch, who is in the middle of a *tough* breakup, manifested just to cheer herself up)! Are y'all holding up okay?" is in order. It shows that you know they wish *just as much as you do* that the plane from Newark wasn't being adorably and permanently damaged as the most precious behemoth holds it between Volkswagen-size paws and furiously double-kicks it.

🐚 The question "If you were me, what would you do?" can come in very handy here. It can be used to assess if you should just call it and head to an airport hotel, or stick around, or what.

Time to get on the plane! I'm always curious about the people who are in *such a rush* to get on the plane that they line up weeks ahead of time in their designated boarding group area; unless your carry-on is massive and simply cannot be gate-checked, enjoy a leisurely sit-and-phone charge during this time. When it is your

"Should you chance accidentally to overhear a remark to your disadvantage, consider first if there may not be some truth in it. If you feel that there is, turn it to profitable account, and try to improve, or to get rid of the fault, whatever it may be."

—Miss Leslie is not interested in your EXCUSES nor your HURT FEELINGS.

time to get on the plane, do have that boarding pass ready to go, smile, and say thank you.

Oh, ho! Seatmates! Here they are! Lizzie Post has a *fabulous* suggestion about how to tease out exactly who these people are and whether they wish to talk to you during every moment of this 7-hour flight.

"You always want to question—am I trapping this person?" Lizzie said, and certainly being strapped onto an uncomfortable chair and repeatedly discouraged from moving is the very definition of trapped. When Lizzie gets on a plane, she floats a little conversational weather balloon.

"You really want to take the temperature of the person next to you," she said. "I say hi as we buckle ourselves in, and I'll say, 'Is this a trip home for you?' and the level to which they answer that question gives me a good indication of whether they are a chatty person."

If, she said, you get the entire story about how it was a visit to a sister, who *had* been estranged for a long time *but* now, ever since Dad died, everything has been different, but the toughest thing about the visit was leaving behind her iguana breeding business, and you wouldn't *believe* what the male iguanas got up to once out of supervision . . . ! Then you have it.

I am the kind of person who is always *beside myself* when strangers want to share dark family secrets and the intricacies of an all-consuming occupation/hobby ("So how *do* you know the females are in heat? Wow. Oh, mannnnn. How many couches *do* they ruin in a given year? Woof, that is a *lot* of couches! Who knew?") But you may not be. If so, Lizzie said, it is *absolutely positively acceptable* to refuse to be held as a conversational hostage.

"I'll say something like, 'Oh! Well, I hope your return trip is really nice. I'm going to tuck into my book now, but do let me know if you need to get up," she said, adding that this is a great way to shut down nonconsensual conversations well.

"You can always say, 'It's been nice chatting with you! I'm going to use this time to write my report,' or whatever," she said.

No matter what you do, please do not give other passengers Mean Looks for things they can't help. If it's a decision they've made—to have that fifth drink and yell loudly, then yes. If their crime is making your flight slightly less comfortable by having a baby who does not understand why its head hurts so bad or being someone who is not, physically, your ideal seatmate,🍍 then back off. You are more than welcome to think, "Hoo! I really and truly wish that baby would stop screaming!" and perhaps even mentally prepare for your dramatic reenactment for whoever picks you up at the airport. You may not, ever, once, signal to this person that you are angry about something they have zero ability to change. And this is why one should always fly with earplugs. They are tiny and weightless and can squish into any shape!

If you, like me, are frightened of hurtling through the air, I have two suggestions.

One, never underestimate the power of sedatives! Frankly, between being someone who is constantly on the verge of panic attacks/crying silently/biting into a toilet paper roll in the bathroom to muffle my own screaming . . . or being a sedate, calm houseplant who just wants to read Harry Potter and reflect on how life has been satisfying and good to her, I know which one I choose. Talk to your doctor!

Two, let the flight crew🍍🍍 know. When I get a moment, say, if I'm boarding and am stopped with one near me, I'll ask, "Do you expect this to be a turbulent flight? I'm a pretty fearful flier."

Oh, my God, I love flight crews so much. They are *so* badass.

🍍 The ideal seatmate: a pug without gas! Or someone who is literally pug-size, but wasn't a baby and didn't cry. Anyone larger than that, which is all of us, is going to intrude on our neighbors during this Sky Voyage of the Damned.

🍍🍍 Or, as I call them, the Psychiatrists of the Sky! Standing between me and plane insanity.

They are people who are trained to get a hundred people evacuated in 90 seconds, or to wrench open a fuselage door while upside down. They are also trained for—you guessed it!—nervous fliers! If you let them know, they will let you know exactly what *they* are expecting for the flight, so you will know that, over Ohio, if it's bumpy, no one is afraid and nothing is wrong because *this was always part of the plan.*

Air time. Sit as quietly as possible. If you're one of those wizards who can go to sleep at will, do that. Do not get drunk and, if you went the sedative route, *please* do not do what I did once, which is to have a couple drinks and do a one-woman reenactment of that scene from *Bridesmaids,* then the next day have to tweet an apology to the wonderful Portland-based flight crew of Alaska Airlines. Y'all didn't deserve that, and I'm so sorry.

On the ground! If you have an *actual* reason for needing to be off the plane, like a tight connection, as opposed to the very natural desire that *everyone on the airplane shares* to get off and move your legs, then let a flight attendant know ahead of time so that she or he may smooth your path off the plane. Otherwise, practice patience. You will be off the plane. Perhaps you'll be off the plane up to 7 *minutes* after the first people are off the plane. But this is a fact of life, as unchangeable as the sunrise, and just as you do not get annoyed at the sun, do not let these confluences of time and physics irk you.

Then, grab your bags, head outside, tongue-kiss the ground, and never get on a plane again.

Huzzah! You have emerged from your journey, whether short or Odyssean, physically, emotionally, and spiritually unscathed. But before work, coffee.

Here, we encounter the nonessential long line, and there are only two options.

Essential long lines being for things like the DMV, kidney transplants, or bread from the *only* store that is open after Hurricane Katrina. Contrary to what your brain may tell you, coffee is a nonessential.

A BRIGHT THOUGHT ABOUT CUSTOMER SERVICE

Nora introduced an idea that I *absolutely love*. Imagine the world is your very own beautiful boutique, and you are striving to give everyone in it a wonderful customer service experience. Because think, for a moment, how great service feels, and think about being able to give that to *everyone*.

More importantly, when you are doing this, you are being *of service*. Being of service is . . . well, it's everything. It's better than anything else that I've tried at feeling sane and happy.

"Saying hello and goodbye to people is really important," she said. "When you're growing up, everyone is so insistent on please and thank you, and of course I think they're very important, too.

"Acknowledging that someone exists is something that makes people say, 'Okay, that girl just walked in the door and acknowledged my presence and said in it a happy, cheerful way, and I'm *not* invisible, I'm a person,' and then the whole time you have with that person, no matter how short or long that is, it's a better feeling and relationship that you have.

"When you walk into a store or restaurant, [employees] always say hello to you, either because they're nice people or they're being paid to do that or

1. Decide that it's not worth it and go elsewhere.

2. Decide that it *is* worth it and then practice good line behavior. This means not cutting, and being generous if someone has stepped out of line for only a moment. This is also paying attention to how the line is moving and where your proper place in it is. By all means, work on your proof of Fermat's Last Theorem or play Candy Crush; deploy whatever self-soothing tools you have in

both, and I think you should greet everyone in the same way. Saying hello to people shows that you're equals."

Sidebar to the Sidebar!

It just so happened that a day after writing that, I listened to two people on a podcast discussing how, as introverts, they *hate* and *dread* the moment a store greeter greets them, and they do everything possible to avoid this interaction. So, y'know, read body language and clues!

For example! Upon encountering someone with headphones on, staring at the ground, one should never bend at the hips, extend the torso toward the withdrawn person's stomach, crane one's neck upward to peer at them from around their own navel, and shout, "Hello!"

If someone is clearly doing their own thing, *obviously let them be.*

If you *did* do this, which obviously you should *not*, then I certainly hope you will e-mail me footage. Footage that I will *never* receive because there will be no footage because you won't do this because #boundaries! Maybe just once, to someone you know. But *just the once.*

your arsenal, but do not let these shift your focus too far away from your main tasks: shuffling along at the proper moments and being ready with your form of payment *and* order when you reach the counter. If you have yet to decide on what you want to purchase and the line is short, then you are not ready to queue!

There is always that terribly awkward moment right after you are handed change when it seems like you really absolutely *must* put your change away, *but* you are also blocking the person behind you, *and* all of a sudden this is less like a commercial transaction and more like the climax of an action movie. WILL SHE DISMANTLE THAT BOMB IN TIME?!?!?!

Take comfort in the fact that this is uncomfortable for everyone, that you are not the only person in the world with this problem, and that if it really, *truly* bothers you, then you can always put your wallet away after offering payment, then clutch change, cards, and or receipts in your hand until you are safely out of the flow.

Office Time

I shall not go deeply here into the intricacies of office life, as so many parts will be addressed elsewhere; for particulars on tough situations, negotiations, and standing up for yourself, please turn to Chapter 3. But below are some sample conversations for making sure that your encounters have a base level civility and productivity to them.

"*Good morning, Coworker Who Is Also in Morning Casual Mode! Did you have fun over the long holiday weekend? Oh, how wonderful! Seeing the Steens Mountain sounds fantastic; any good tips? Dying to go!*"

"*Hello, Calm Coworker! How are you? Today I want to finish up X and I'll be needing Y from you, ideally by around noon—is that possible? Wonderful!*"

"*Hi, Busy-Looking Coworker. I know you're slammed so I'll be quick. Any chance I could grab X project from you by 2:00, or if not, do you have a good ETA on it? Thank you!*"

"*Hey,*" and a nod is all you need to give to a coworker who is clearly frantic and in a rush and you can do nothing to help.

"*Oh my gosh, Linda! Can I help you with that?*" is a fantastic thing to say to a coworker who is clearly frantic if you can help out. If they are the type who hates being helped, then don't. If they are the type who hates feeling like they're inconveniencing other people, then just silently begin gathering up papers/rounding up the M&Ms that have rolled everywhere/sweeping up the broken remains of the office ant farm.

When you leave a voice mail, it should sound something like this:

"*Good morning! This is Kelly Williams Brown calling from My House. It's Monday morning, and I am trying to reach Pork-chop Pat at the deli counter to see if you have that prosciutto I eat straight from the package available. I'd love to get a call back by this afternoon if possible; my drop-dead time for prosciutto is Tuesday at 11:00 a.m. If Pat could call me back as soon as he's able, I would be so grateful. My phone number is 555-HAM-NOWW. Once again, that is (slower) 5-5-5 (beat) H-A-M (beat) N-O-W-W, and this is Kelly Williams Brown calling from My House in regard to prosciutto. Thank you, bye-bye!*"🍍

This was my best-practices voice-mail procedure when I was in the newsroom. It says who I am immediately, where I am calling from, when, whom I want to reach, and why. It lets the receiver know what kind of timetable I am hoping for and at which point the message is no longer valid. It gives the number twice, because

🍍 I could not tell you why, but almost every single gracious lady I would interview would end things with a chirpy "Bye-bye!" And I thought, Huh, that is odd. Could I pull that off? So I tried it and it felt right. Felt *real* right. Bye-bye!

sometimes people mess it up the first time, *and* it ends with my name, because sometimes by the time people have listened to a long message, they forgot the name at the beginning, and I don't want them to have to play it again.

Lunchtime! Perhaps you are eating at your desk, in which case, please be aware of smells and mouth noises, which can be quite . . . noticeable to some. If you are heading out and do not want company, go to town! Politely deflect any invitations quickly and honestly, "You're so sweet to ask, but not today. Thank you!"

If you are going out with those coworkers, please be aware of who is going and how conspicuously these plans are being made. It

Theories of Grace

Some people say to be gracious is to have good manners, but I think it goes further. To be gracious is to be sincerely compassionate.

I'm sincere about being polite and listening to you and caring for you and extending hospitality not just to be the gracious host but because that's what you do—you extend it for others. It's about learning. Because if it's just something you're taught, that's not true graciousness.

It's our subconscious love. Maybe we're just going through life to come out on the other side with compassion.

Dominic and I have been married 47 years, and I often think about certainly being as polite to my husband and to my family as I would be to a stranger or anyone else. Dominic is always so pleasant when he gets up in the morning. It doesn't matter what's on his mind, his plate, his shoulders—he's always so polite.

You learn a calmness. You learn to watch your thoughts and your

is absolutely and totally acceptable to not want to spend your hour of freedom with every single one of your coworkers, particularly that one who always somehow makes everything feel inappropriately sexual.

It is *not* kind (or appropriate) to be a part of a clique that clearly announces itself. This just hurts feelings. An e-mail chain is the perfect medium for this invitation; if it *is* a vocal, "I'm going to Beautiful Burrito Land!" then try to follow it with "Does anyone want to come along or place an order?" Secret lunch bunches should quietly congregate at the elevator or even outside the building. Think sex in an airplane bathroom strategy: Timing is slightly staggered and no one should pick up on

Beverly Gianna

words, to think before you speak and remain calm.

Perhaps you've had a horrible day and you come home and encounter chaos—well, don't engage in that chaos! Remain calm. Remain at peace. That's what you keep in your head every hour and every minute—peace begins with me.

I don't necessarily reach out to others when I'm having hard times as much as I used to, because I think the only person who can change your perception or yourself, for that matter, is you. I have learned to calm myself and go inward.

I'm not at all put off at anybody wanting to help—that's fine! I embrace anyone who embraces me. But it's not necessarily that I require it from someone else. You don't find your strength, your real core, in someone else.

the fact that these people are all going to the same place for the same purpose.

Note: For more on e-mail communication, please see page 50 of Chapter 2.

Whilst out with your coworkers, you may enjoy a good complaining session about work and the various personalities contained therein. But do be careful, and please remember that the person who always has and shares the juicy gossip is not terribly likely to decide that *you* are the one person whose actions, anecdotes, and thoughts will be kept classified.

This is also a wonderful time to expound upon the art of the Southern Insult, which is just about my favorite thing. Let's say that your coworker Larry never, ever, ever does a goddamn thing and instead expends a ton of energy doing everything possible to *avoid* work. [img] This shared frustration may indeed be commented upon! Here's how it goes: faint nice thing, thing that, if repeated, sounds innocuous enough but with vocal intonation is clearly anything but faint nice thing. Here we go; translation in footnotes.

"Y'all? So Larry, who, bless his heart, [img] is *so* nice? Yes, Larry Slotherson, he seems a little . . . *(pause for emphasis, grimace briefly) forgehhhtful!* [img] I have *definitely* had to ask the poor lamb [img] for that contact number *18 times now,* and he

---

[img] These people are totally mystifying. Let us accept them as an unchangeable feature of this planet, like tar fires that burn eternally in Kazakhstan.

[img] *Bless his heart* = I will murder him. The angrier you are, the more you may draw out the "t" on hearttttttttttttttttttttttttttt.

[img] *Forgetful* = He's either lazy, a complete idiot, purposefully holding out for reasons known only to his awful self, or a combination of all of the above. Other good adjectives here could be "popular," "witty," "confused," "doing his best."

[img] *Poor lamb* = *!?%face.

still hasn't gotten it to me. Do you think he needs some help?🍍 Awww, but he's trying *so hard,*🍍🍍 I think!"🍍🍍🍍

Now. Should this get back to Mr. Slotherson, here is what you said: He seems a little forgetful. You might be able to help him out. He is trying hard.

You see, this, if and when repeated, is much less damning than saying he's an idiot who refuses to lift a finger and, consequently, is making your life a million times harder than it needs to be.

When you are unavailable, either for a short period or a 3-week vacation, let others who will need you know ahead of time; also let them know the best way to reach you (if possible) and when things will be back to normal. This could even be a very quick e-mail to the people on your team:

> *Hello, Allyson, Elisabeth, Paul, Alex, Jack, and Sarah Jane,*
>
> *Just a heads-up that I'm putting my head down and stepping away from e-mail until I can get XYZ done, hopefully around 3:00 this afternoon. If you really need something between now and then, ping me on Slack or just poke your head in?*
>
> *Cheers, I hate this project but at least I can see the finish line,*
>
> *Kelly*

🍍 *Do you think he needs some help?* = If I have to ask once more, it will come as a Post-it adhered to his cubicle with a stiletto knife.

🍍🍍 *He's trying so hard* = Any reasonably intelligent human would not be struggling with this, the same way reasonably intelligent people don't struggle with operating a standard toilet in good working order.

🍍🍍🍍 He is *not* trying hard and we all know it and here you are giving the tiniest shadow of a doubt that perhaps something truly terrible is going on with Larry, some family illness or crisis of conscience or *whatever* that would justify this egregious abdication of responsibility that *isn't even that hard.* C'mon LARRY, we are all on the same team here.

Then, if and when someone interrupts with a nonessential thing, you may brightly say, "Hi, Joseph! I want to help with this [inane tiny problem]. I'm on a tight deadline for this presentation; may I check in to see if you still need help when it's done around 3:00?" In this way, you acknowledge that someone needs you, that you know what they want, that you are not able to help them at that very moment, and that help *will* be available, but not this minute.

If they persist—and it doesn't seem truly urgent—listen diligently, nod, then repeat, in precisely the same tone: "May I help you with this around 3:00?"

Oh, dear! Inscrutable Boss has poked her head in!

"Sooooo . . . okay, I really wanted for the . . . thing . . . you've been working on to be . . . different," she says. You know each word is layered with meaning, and yet have absolutely no idea what that meaning could be. Put on your verbal Sherlock Holmes hat!

"Hi, Melisstery! ❀ *So, I want to make sure we're on the same page, and I am sorry you had to ask about this. By 'thing,' do you mean 'presentation'? Oh, my insurance paperwork! Sorry for that confusion. So, right now, my insurance paperwork is filled out and with HR. What would you like me to do? Go take it away from HR, fold each sheet into a tiny sailboat, then . . . ? Release those sailboats into the Willamette River, and . . . ? Okay. Absolutely. So sometime between now and the Ides of March, I'm going take them, fold them, then give each one a tiny stick mast, go to the river, light the masts on fire, quietly chant a Queen song of my choice* ❀❀ *then watch them until I can no longer see the small flames? Perfect. Thank you so much! My hands are pretty full until next week, but it will absolutely be done by . . . let's say March 12th? That gives us a nice 3-day window."*

❀ It is *hard* to come up with a female name that sounds like mystery, y'all. I tried. Know that I tried.

❀❀ "Fat Bottomed Girls," obviously, should *always* be your Queen song of choice. "Killer Queen" is a close second.

> "When visiting a fancy-store with a gentleman, refrain from excessively admiring any handsome or expensive article you may chance to see there. Above all, express no wish that you were able to buy it, and no regret that you cannot, lest he should construe those extreme tokens of admiration into hints that you wish him to buy it for you."

—Like Kanye, Miss Leslie abhors a gold digger.

In no way is your vocal tone or face implying that every word out of her mouth is a madness-inducing Zen koan, with endless interpretations meant to be puzzled through over a lifetime.

You are teasing out the bits of information, without judgment, to figure out the what, where, and how of what she wants, with an interested yet calm expression, nodding as she reveals each logistically insane detail.

As for the why, well, with confusing people, this is a Pandora's box. Depending on the person's authority over your professional life, you don't always need to *know* why she wants you to give your insurance paperwork a Viking funeral. As my friend Hanna would say, we don't get all the answers, and we shouldn't necessarily go looking for them; they will come or they won't. So long as your understanding of logistics and next steps are clear, you have shared this understanding with her, and she agrees, you are *on the same page and that is all that counts.*

Working, working, never shirking, never having any kind of personal conversation on company electronics—this is the gracious way! Saying hello and goodbye and wishing people a nice weekend and if you *know* they are going through a tough time, looking them in the eyes and asking them how they are, *unless* they are clearly trying to hold it together and/or are in a very public office spot— this is the way of the gracious worker!

Quittin' time! Workin' for the weekend! Blowin' this popsicle stand! Take a moment to gather all materials carefully, make notes of what you need to do tomorrow, particularly those small things you might otherwise forget, and maybe, if you know one of your coworkers is really struggling, take a moment to write them a sweet Post-it note and leave it on their keyboard to brighten their morning. In fact, kind little notes to coworkers are almost always a good idea, and I highly recommend them as a matter of course in your working environment.

These small things mean something. Once, I worked at an ad agency on a big project as a freelancer. Everyone else on the team had been working together for months, and so I felt a little left out. One morning, during the toughest part of the project, I arrived to find a tiny carved stone coyote on my keyboard with a note from the designer; everyone had gotten one from her. I still have that little coyote.

Give people little coyotes, 🍍 because work can be a frustrating and unfriendly place. Give them coyotes because you spend more time with them than you do with your loved ones. Give them coyotes so they *know* that you see them, that you appreciate them, that you could not do your job without them.

Entering the Leisure and Pleasure Zone!

Beautiful freedom! Your time is yours, and yours alone, to pursue arcane hobbies or meditate under a tree, to spend in *exactly the way you see fit!*

Ha-ha, just kidding! Actually, if you are my kind of champion hermit, then your evening plans do, in fact, consist of bingeing *Orange Is the New Black* while practicing calligraphy and avoiding text messages. In this instance, all you need to do is be thoughtful on the ride home and then be *so ding-dang gracious to yourself! INTO THAT BATHTUB! Eat a calzone in there! Who caaaaaaaaares? Push back against naysayers who would tell you that soup is definitely not an appropriate tub food. Screw conventional wisdom! Live every bit of yourself and do not apologize.*

🍍 I am using "little coyote" as a *metaphor;* no need to go to the Santa Fe gift shop in your town.

Buuuuut, more than likely, your evening involves (sigh) *other people*. People whom you love! Like friends or family! And though you may be tired after a long day of work, if you have made these plans, then they must be followed through *without* flaking.

Oof, I am so flaky. I am famously flaky. There is a distinct curvature to my desire to get together socially that is in play if I am even slightly tired/cranky (see flaky chart).

However, this curvature has *absolutely nothing to do* with the fact that friends and family, who are *not* flaky, are looking forward to these plans that I proposed and they agreed to. Plus, 9 times out of 10, when I actually arrive, it's a blast. If it's not and I really am feeling down/exhausted/like I am poor company in a group situation, I can leave after about 45 minutes. If it's one-on-one, then perhaps a warning ahead of time is best, maybe a text containing a mutually enjoyable, lower-key suggestion.

"Hanna, I'm so excited to see you, but I have to warn you that it's been a hell of a week at work and I'm feeling a little low energy. Instead of going to that indoor trampoline complex, could we do a glass of wine at Nice Quiet Wine Bar? Dying to see you, but I'm not sure I have any double backflips in me tonight."

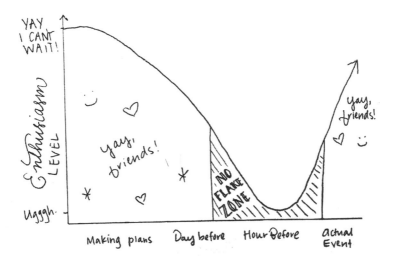

Now! At this point, Hanna may respond in kind, that she too is exhausted, and let's do a rain check or that the wine bar sounds perfect. This works for everyone! However, if Hanna gives even the *slightest* hesitation, then it means that her heart was really and truly set on trampolining. At this point, the gracious thing to do is text back.

"Perfect—let's stick with the original plan. Can't wait!" perhaps with a few positive emojis.

Ah, here we are! All together! Except for that one friend who, as a matter of course, is always 45 minutes late to everything! Please don't be that friend. If you need to lie to yourself, as I do, to arrive anywhere on time, then just pretend that everything starts 30 minutes early. If you are always late, it means you do not have a super-phenomenal grasp on how time and logistics play out in your life. It's okay. Me, too.

"Punctuality is *extremely* important," Lizzie said. "You never, ever want to start an interaction with an apology."

Because when you start with an apology, you are *immediately* asking others to forgive you and let go of their (perhaps quite reasonable) annoyance, and, yes, making it about you.

When possible, I give a *later* time than I think I am actually available. If I have a work call at 5:30 that I expect to run an hour, that does not mean to make plans for 6:45. If I *think* it will take me 15 to 30 minutes to tidy up, leave the office, get in my car, and arrive at the second location, I *decide* that it will actually take an hour. Therefore, I can make a plan for 7:30.

This means that I am not arriving in a rush, clambering in with soot on my face, which is

> "However smart and witty you may be considered, do not exercise your wit in rallying and bantering your friends. If you do so, their friendship will soon be worn out, or converted into positive enmity."
>
> —Miss Leslie, on why mean funny people are great to be around . . . for 10 minutes

weird because I don't remember being in a coal mine but I clearly was, I'm not out of breath, and—this is so key—I can just say hello and join the gathering like a normal person.

Lizzie suggests that we nonpunctuals should start timing ourselves: How long, exactly, does it take to go from a total state of rest to ready to walk out the door? And yes, stop the timer when you are *in the car*, not when you walk out the door, because I have an average of 1.5 return trips to the house to get whatever I've forgotten.

If the tardiness is small—less than 15 minutes—a text is just perfect.

"I'm so sorry, but traffic is terrible and I'm running a little late. Please go ahead and sit down and order! And, if you feel like it, maybe ask for a glass of vinho verde for me?" Do this, Lizzie says, *as soon as you know you are going to be late.*

Being A Good Customer

Ah, Nice Quiet Wine Bar! The best! And here comes the server. Anyone who has waited tables may skip this section, because y'all already know, but for those who haven't . . .

- Your server is (surprise!) a human being and therefore entitled to certain things. Smile, say hello, if they give their name, try to remember it. In a relaxed atmosphere, you may certainly ask how the night is going. If they are in Frantic Server Mode, then everyone will be most pleased to get straight to business.

- Take cues from them and perhaps take a glance around: How many tables are they serving, and how many other waiters are here? If the answer is "all of the tables, because there aren't any

---

Key signs: darting eyes, saying things as quickly and clearly as possible, nodding to the patron across the restaurant who is doing the Angry Penguin rigid posture/frowny look move

other waiters," then what a perfect opportunity for patience and understanding!

- Make sure that everyone is actually ready to order when it's time. If not, asking for just another minute is quite fine. No one need rush in this place of banqueting and pleasure!

- If you find you need something—say, sweetener for your iced tea—it's thoughtful to collect these requests in advance. A quick "Y'all? I'm going to ask Douggles the Waiter for some sugar, does anyone else need anything?" is the difference between Douggles making one trip and Douggles making three, as everyone else slowly realizes that they, too, need something.

- Alas! You asked for crab claws, and yet darlin' Douggles has brought you a big bowl of steamed rice. No need to apologize, for you've done nothing wrong—there is a small error that was somehow made, it's not the end of the world, this will be resolved. "Hello! (gently touch steamed rice mountain) I actually ordered the crab claws. May I trade you? Thank you!" Never a bad time to say thank you to someone who is at times literally running back and forth to meet your and your friends' needs.

- If you need Douggles's assistance, then you may certainly make eye contact with him and very lightly raise two fingers. You should not, however, stop him while he is schlepping an armful of dirty dishes. Think about the last time your arms were full of plates; are you receptive and attentive in this moment?

- Ideally, everyone has brought cash. If they haven't, please pay in as simple and straightforward a way as possible. If this is an invitation *you* issued to a friend, then please offer to take the check.

- If you *know* that you owe this person a meal *and* you know that there will be a scramble to grab the check, then by all means, slip Douggles your card ahead of time.

- If they are dying to pay, say no at least twice before accepting their generosity.

"Your server is not your servant, and I rarely dine out with friends who treat servers like they are," Lizzie said. "It's one thing to express that things haven't gone well, but you need to be careful not to take it out on the server—they don't have anything to do with your food being cooked the wrong way."

Tip whatever is standard, and away you whirl, off into a night filled with possibility!

Traversing the city with friends is just the right time to practice physical grace and attentiveness. Though you may feel heady with wine, joy, and the perfect company, though you may know in your very bones that this city—nay, this *world*—belongs to y'all, though your laughter echoes down canyons of skyscrapers; instead of fading away with the distance, it will become louder. These laughs will amplify far beyond you; they will ricochet off these beautiful buildings forever because you *are* this city, bitch.

But, surprise! I don't care how young and vital and *alive* you are; you still only get 40 percent of the sidewalk.

For there are both humans coming the opposite direction and—this is key—perhaps someone behind you who is *not* strolling through a warm summer evening, talking and laughing of memories past, but rather is in a *great* hurry because her grandmother is in the hospital and she would really, really like to arrive without delay.

So here is that attentiveness: You are paying attention not only to the members of your group, but also to others in your vicinity, both ahead and behind you. There are obvious safety implications here, too, which I will not go into but—yeah.

In the course of your visual sweep of the scene, note these facts: Is everyone in my group still with the group, or has someone lagged behind and is now struggling to catch back up or, worse yet, is nowhere in sight? Is there someone who seems to be trailing a little *too* close? Is there someone coming up *fast* behind us?

If the answer any question is yes, raise the volume of your voice: "Friends! Hey, Allyson and Meredith? Hold on 1 second. Has anyone seen Cat?/Let's let her by/I need to find something in my bag."

That last one is for stranger danger, but any of these would require moving out of the right of way, perhaps to stand between some parked cars or duck into an alcove.

If any friend is feeling *especially* festive after the evening and perhaps is finding walking to be a tall order, maybe you offer your arm? Not like, "Hey! You're DRUNK, I'm not, you need to control yourself," but "Sarah! I love you so. Come here, kitten, and walk with me!"

Of course, it may be that everyone you are with *totally* understands all these things implicitly, and there is no need to do a thing. But if not, just consider yourself the gracious sheepdog of the group. When requests for movement are made, they are either *directly* couched in an explanation of why or are spoken not as an indictment of someone's behavior but rather an exclamation of love followed by a desire to walk *right* next to them.

Home again, home again, jiggety jig! 🍍

How wonderful it is to have survived this day! There were no snakes laying their leathery egg sacs in your desk drawer! No one fell into an open street grate and required surgery! Your friends and family are all safe, and so are you! You *didn't even step on a slug barefoot!* A moment of gratitude is in order. Nothing fancy, just a deep inhale, a brief recollection of the good things that happened today, of the larger circumstances of your life, and exhale.

Be gracious to your face and teeth via nighttime routine, do whatever it is that you do when you get home, and if you have it in you, check tomorrow's weather. Then look through your clothing and decide what you shall wear to face whatever tomorrow brings, knowing that, if nothing else, at least you will have this fabulous dress on.

Last thing in bed at night, before you close your eyes, go

🍍 This is something that I say with a slightly embarrassing regularity, but before I put it in print forever I did a quick Google to make sure this isn't a small part of some horrific racist nursery rhyme because . . . well, you just never know. Anyway, per Wikipedia, the beginning part is "To market, to market, to buy a fat pig; home again, home again, jiggity jig!" Also, it's from 1598, so there is almost certainly *something* awful in there, but I couldn't find it.

through the day in a bit more depth: What were the wonderful things? What were the not-so-wonderful things, and how did I handle them? What am I grateful for? When did I do my absolute best, and what did that look and feel like? When did I not do my best; what did *that* look and feel like? What do I know now that I didn't know this morning, and how can I remember and use it to be good and kind and helpful?

One last thank-you to the universe, then close your eyes, you wondrous creation, you. Please, have the loveliest dreams.

Conclusion

Go Be Gracious, Y'all

Well, there you have it! That's it! Every last thing there is to say about graciousness, manners, etiquette, and how to be a good human being!

I am, of course, kidding. This is an infinite topic that we all could spend the rest of our lives discussing, and I hope we do because this world needs all the grace we can summon.❋

Because—at least to me—this is the Big Question. Maybe the only one. Forget about the meaning of life; forget about what happens next. Well, or don't, as long as you know that you may never have a satisfactory answer. But you know what can be answered? Every day? The questions of how we treat one another, how we expect to be treated, what is and is not acceptable. In short, each day we decide who we are and what we will do.

It is moving through life, as Dorothy Buckhanan Wilson does, with an aim to leave good things behind her, to make every interaction, no matter how brief, one that she and the other party are both

❋ We could have the BEST dialogues that stretch through the decades, with elders and newcomers and definitely hors d'oeuvres. We'd take breaks only to refresh our beverages, laugh really hard, and sometimes, take quick chaise longue naps when our minds reel from the brilliant, shimmering politeness.

grateful for. It is anchoring yourself to the knowledge that when you think of others instead of yourself, your world automatically gets bigger and happier. It is celebrating the pleasures of life, whether it's coffee or a huge gala, and it's weathering the unspeakable sorrows that we are each, at some point, called to wade through with our heads held high.

Every single time you make the decision to be gracious, you have done . . . well, I would say your fair share, but that implies, again, that all this is something we have to do. We don't. We get to do it. We get to move forward in time and space scattering patience and kindness and compassion behind us like flower seed, while knowing that we may not ever see that flower open its face to the sun.

And like that flower, we get to turn our faces toward the sun. We could, if we wanted, focus on anger, sadness, our own pains, and resentments. Or we can turn again and again toward appreciating what is good and beautiful in the people around us, which we only see when we look outward with openness. We are not here to be bitter; we are not here to be petty; we are not here to do things half-assed. We're here to love and celebrate our time on earth with the people in our lives, because we could *all* get hit by that proverbial bus any moment. What do you want to be remembered for when you are not here?

As drag superstar Katya put it, "When I look back at my life, I would actually rather, in my heart of hearts, hope to see that I consistently treated people with respect, that I gave positivity regardless of the situation, that I was kind. *That* is more of a legacy than being a legendary art star. Not everyone can be an art star, but *everyone* can be a good person."

The heart of graciousness is compassion. It's attention to those around you, whether they are your favorite person in the world or that person trying to get by you on the sidewalk. It's kindness, and most of all, it's giving love to those around you.

You will do it in your own way, whatever that is, and not spend a moment lamenting that your way is not another's way. We all come into this world with gifts, and what a waste to spend a *second* thinking that you should be someone other than who you are.

So, please, take whatever you found useful in here and leave the rest, and go forth knowing that every kindness and compassion you show to the world makes it—and you—just that much better, happier, lovelier.

All my love,

Kelly

Acknowledgments

My gratitude is so damn big. I'm not talking skyscraper big, I'm talking Pacific Ocean big, scientific notation big, "I put off writing this page until literally the last minute because it terrified me" big. There is a zero percent chance you'd be holding this book without dozens of people, all of whom I am going to try to list here, at least one of whom I am going to forget and hope will forgive me, and all of whom are responsible for the brilliant and the true; any errors are mine and mine alone.

First, editors Leah Miller and Anna Cooperberg each deserve a firstborn child at *minimum*; they are so terribly thoughtful, smart, wise, and patient and I love both of them. Ditto Brandi Bowles, who gives naught but the very finest of counsel and edits; a living model of what it means to be an International Businesswoman of Fearsome Elegance and Competence. When she and Dana Spector walk in formation, the literary and entertainment industries tremble under their footsteps. Hanna Thompson, I'm still in awe of your organizational prowess! Emily Westcott, you were a deus ex machina and in ten years we'll all be working for you...or dead by your hands.

I will never forget the day I walked into a meeting at Rodale and sat down at a table of scary-smart, fearless women; if you find a more generous, supportive publisher out there, *be careful!* It's probably a hologram and/or trap. Special thanks to senior project editor Hope Clarke and copy editor Nancy Bailey—they caught everything and their competence allows *me* to sleep at night even as I kept *them* up with endless revisions. Christina Gaugler designed the inside of this book and made it so gorgeous despite my thwarting her at every turn by blowing lettering deadlines. The outside of this book is beautiful thanks to William Bragg, my OTP photog; Willyum Beck, who styled it just right; and Liz Gross plus the Xtabay Vintage family, who dressed me and let me shoot in their shop. Amy King designed a cover that I can only describe as Perf McGurf. Every week, hopping on the phone with Susan Turner, Emily Weber Eagan, and Angie Giammarino was the besttttt; their willingness to expend such time and talent to tell the world about this book is everything. Finally, this team thrives under the incredible leadership of editorial director Jennifer Levesque and publisher Gail Gonzales; they create the most fertile of ground and it makes me ugly-yet-happy cry that I get to be on a team with all y'all.

Without so many women (and men!) willing to explain their personal magic, this book would be ten pages long. Thank you, thank you, thank you to Bonnie Trumbull, Nora Foran and her mother Mary Jane Murrell, Marion Hutchins, Chris and Alan Gluck, Virginia Provosty, Lelia Gowland, Frankie Bell, Lizzie Post, Nancy Kaffer, Dorothy Buckhanan Wilson, Rabbi Rami M. Shapiro, Sarah Von Bargen, Alexandra Franzen, Sheila Hamilton, Alex Angel, Lee Weinstein, Rev. Dr. Brian Baker, Daniel Post Senning, Mary Nixon Johnson, Dr. Holly B. Rogers, international drag superstar KATYA, Beverly Gianna, Kate Gremillion, Susan Mancuso, Holly Shumway, and Brendan Boyle.

I wrote this through some of the very hardest and darkest times of my life, made bearable only because of the immense love and grace of friends and family. All the thanks to Jessica Maxwell and Tom Andersen; Kirk Kindle and Tammie Hammett and Janine for such wonderful shelter. My friends who listened to me say the same thing ten thousand times and told me I'd be okay—Anne, Elisabeth, Kim, Schulte, Meredith, Molly, Jess, Sarah Jane, Jack, Paul, Chris, Steve, Hannah, Kate. To my family—Fahja, Mamma Bean and Seesters Olivia and Elizabeth, and Dave and Elle Belle.

Finally, Al—you are grace embodied, and it's just right that this book was born with you around.

Cat—you are not only the best *Confidential Literary Secretary* evah, you are also astonishingly loving and giving; someday I shall successfully wife you.

Index

Underscored page references indicate boxed text.